Seek Sobriety
Find Serenity

SEEK
SOBRIETY
FIND
SERENITY

Thoughts for Every Day

RABBI ABRAHAM J.
TWERSKI, M.D.

PHAROS BOOKS

A SCRIPPS HOWARD COMPANY

NEW YORK

First published in 1993.

Library of Congress Cataloging-in-Publication
Data
Twerski, Abraham J.
    Seek sobriety, find serenity : thoughts for
every day / Abraham J. Twerski.
        p.   cm.
    ISBN 0-88687-735-0
    1. Twelve-step programs—Religious
aspects—Meditations.   2. Devotional
calendars.   I. Title.
BL624.5.T85   1993
291.4'3—dc20   92-39036   CIP

Printed in the United States of America

Pharos Books
A Scripps Howard Company
200 Park Avenue
New York, NY 10166

10 9 8 7 6 5 4 3 2 1

Pharos Books are available at special discounts
on bulk purchases for sales promotions,
premiums, fundraising or educational use. For
details, contact the Special Sales Department,
Pharos Books, 200 Park Avenue, New York,
NY 10166

INTRODUCTION
❦

In 1985, it occurred to me that telephone messages on a variety of subjects were available to people, and that there might be some benefit to making a message about sobriety and recovery readily available to interested persons. Gateway Rehabilitation Center then publicized *Dial-A-Sober-Thought*, offering weekly inspirational messages on recovery topics.

This public service was extremely well received. For example, one woman wrote, "One night I was extremely agitated. I awoke at 2 AM with an intense urge to drink. My sponsor was out of town, and I was not close enough with anyone else in the program to feel comfortable awakening them at this hour. I called your *Dial-A-Sober-Thought*, and it got me over the hump. In fact, I called that number six times during that night, and although I heard a repetition of the same message six times, it saved my sobriety until I could reach someone the next morning." Many complimentary comments were received, and some people asked for copies of these messages to have them available at all times.

By 1992, we had accumulated enough weekly messages to provide a "sober thought" for each day of the year. This book thus contains these messages, and since the service is continuing, anyone interested in new messages can call 412-928-LIFE (5433). At night or weekend rates, the cost of the call is minimal, and in situations such as described above, where no one else may be readily available, the benefits may be very great.

A theme which repeats itself throughout this book is that concepts that are helpful in recovery from chemical dependency have broad application and can be constructively applied to a wide variety of problems and stresses of everyday life. I therefore hope that although the primary focus of thoughts on sobriety was to assist people in recovery from chemical dependency, these messages will be found to be a value to *all* who seek serenity in life, or in other words, to *everyone*.

—*Rabbi Abraham J. Twerski, M.D.*

Why Start the New Year Numb?
❦

The truly happy New Year's Day is a sober one.

On December 31, people gather at parties, many of them intoxicated with alcohol, and they exclaim "Happy New Year!" It would seem that these people are happy greeting the new year.

Alcohol is used primarily for its anesthetic effects. It makes people feel better because it numbs the distress that they are experiencing, whether it be depression, anxiety, awkwardness, or just being ill at ease. No one ever uses an anesthetic to eliminate good feelings.

If everyone is happy on New Year's Eve, why do they drink so much? As the year draws to a close, people look back and realize, "Another year of my life gone. I am a year older, but not any wiser nor richer, and perhaps even deeper in debt than one year ago." People have experienced disappointments in the past year as some of their expectations failed to materialize. Facing the end of the year may be depressing, and it is this depression that they try to anesthetize with alcohol.

People who have had sobriety during the past year do not need to be anesthetized to greet the new year. They can look back on a period of personal growth because each day was an achievement, bringing new strength and skills. A year of sobriety can be enjoyed with pride.

Dealing With Anger

Some people think that a virtuous person should never be angry. Some psychologists suggest that people should express anger freely, because keeping it pent up can cause neurotic symptoms.

In sobriety we learn how to deal with many emotions. During the active addiction, we either kill all our emotions with chemicals or cast away all inhibitions and act out all our emotions. Neither of these approaches is healthy or tolerable.

There is a difference between feeling and reacting. If someone steps heavily on your toe and you do not *feel* any pain, there must be something wrong. If you have a healthy pain perception, you have a choice of how to react. How you *react* is a matter of choice, but *feeling* the pain is not.

This is also true of anger. If you do not feel anger when provoked, there is something wrong. You may have been programmed to repress anger so that you don't perceive it, and that is unhealthy. If you *do* perceive anger, you have a choice of how to react. With sober judgment, you can decide what the most prudent response is. You may then decide that kicking and screaming will make more noise than sense, and delay your response until you can deliver it with calm, deliberate logic, which gives you a much better chance of getting your point across.

Learning From Loss
❦

How can we best deal with the adversities resulting from addiction?

One recovering woman said, "When I lost so many things that were important to me during my drinking, I was bitter, angry, and rebellious. Now, with a sober mind, I can look back and see that this was God's way of taking away from me those things that I did not have good enough sense to give up myself. I was hanging on for dear life to a job and relationships that were not in my best interests, but in my addiction I could not see this."

People who are years into recovery have stated that they never could have achieved the growth and maturity in any other way. Some have said that although the cost was exorbitant, their character development was worth the steep price they had to pay.

This woman explained that when she suffered the losses, the pain aroused feelings of bitterness, defiance, and anger at God. She probably felt this way as an infant when her mother held her while the physician administered a painful injection to immunize her against dreadful diseases, and only when she matured could she be grateful for this.

In talking to families of people in their addiction, we point out the necessity for "tough love," which must contain both elements: sincere love, and the requisite firmness. Perhaps God, too, practices tough love, and it is only after we recover that we appreciate this.

Growth in Sobriety

Growth in sobriety can provide a feeling of self-worth.

One woman said, "I used to depend on other people to make me feel good inside. When relationships did not meet my expectations, I became emotionally starved. I had nothing inside to sustain me.

"My emotional deprivation made me ravenous for love and attention from others. I would go to desperate lengths to elicit a man's love, giving him my total devotion. When no one gave me the love I wanted, I decided there must be something wrong with me for needing so much and I felt ashamed of my neediness. I was angry at the people who let me down by not providing me with their love, and I felt guilty about being angry. I isolated myself so that no one would discover my neediness and emptiness.

"As I recovered, I accepted my neediness and allowed myself to feel my pain. I became willing to believe that God loved me and would bring happiness into my life if I would let Him. I became willing to learn to love myself as a child of God.

"I realized that God did not give me my needs to use against me, but to enrich my life. God made me a worthwhile person and He saw in me a loving and lovable woman. When I developed faith that God put goodness in me, I knew that if I searched, I would find it."

Family Participation in Recovery
🍎

Addictive behavior can be so distressful that when recovery begins, everyone breathes a sigh of relief.

But things don't always remain this way. Sobriety brings about change, and when a significant change occurs in one member of the family, this calls for some changes in other family members. Changes are seldom easy, and may even constitute formidable challenges— as happens in the case of "promotion sickness," which is a depression that may develop when a person receives a coveted promotion. Similarly, although the addict's ceasing to drink or use chemicals is wonderful, it results in a marked change in the addict's life-style, and it can actually be stressful to all family members.

Sobriety is a process of progressive growth. If the recovering person grows while other people in the family remain stagnant, this disparity can cause problems within the family.

It is, therefore, important that family members share in the recovery process. Sometimes there is resistance on the part of relatives who say, "I never drank or used. Why should I get involved?" Or the addict may not want family members to become involved in the recovery process. Both are serious mistakes. Family involvement, whether it be with Al-Anon, Nar-Anon, or counseling with qualified family therapists, can help family members make the adjustments necessary so that recovery is simpler and more pleasant for all.

Face Sobriety
With Realistic Expectations
❦

What should a person expect from recovery?

One person said, "When I came into recovery, I expected God to open the gates of heaven and let me in. Instead, he opened the gates of hell and let me out." Another person said, "I can now see that my *real* problem was not my *problems*, but my *solutions*."

Some people entering recovery think that when they stop using chemicals everything will be okay. But many people use chemicals to escape from problems with which they feel they are unable to cope. When the escaping stops, the unresolved problems must be confronted, and this may not be an easy task.

Getting sober is not an entrance into heaven, because difficult adjustments and uncomfortable decisions have to be made. It is certainly true that using chemicals creates a hell by aggravating and magnifying problems, yet while people are under the anesthetic effect of those chemicals they may have little awareness of their problems.

Fortunately, the recovery programs help people know that they *do* have the ability to cope with their problems. With proper help, you can find successful solutions. And as newly discovered skills and strengths help you cope more effectively with reality, life does become more manageable, easier, and even quite pleasant.

Growth Requires Courage
🍎

Growth in sobriety may not always be comfortable.

Our grandmothers used to say that some of the discomforts children have are "growing pains." Modern medicine denies this, but our grandmothers knew that growth is rarely without some pain.

How can lobsters grow when they are encased in a rigid and unyielding shell? When the lobster feels compressed, it retreats to a recess in the underwater formations, sheds its old shell, and forms a new, larger one. When it grows to the limits of the new shell, it repeats the process until it reaches its maximum size.

Although the lobster sheds its shell in a protected environment, it is nevertheless defenseless against predatory fish, and is at risk of being dashed against a rock by a sudden rush of water. In order to grow, a lobster must risk its life. It has no other option because, otherwise, it must live in the oppression of its own shell.

Humans do not have to risk their lives in order to grow, but if we do not wish to live under the crushing restraints and oppression of our limitations, we must take some risks in expanding our personalities. Trying new things carries a risk of failure, and we must often put our egos on the line.

People in the recovery fellowships are fortunate in having the safety net of the program, and a trust in a Higher Power. Nevertheless, growth requires courage, and that is why we pray for the courage to change the things we can.

Self-Awareness Brings Self-Improvement
❦

Recovery from chemical dependency requires changing undesirable character traits. Some of the traits in addiction may also occur in people who have not had chemicals problems. Because the latter may never reach a crisis that forces them to change, they might maintain these traits throughout life. In this sense, the recovering person actually has a distinct advantage over the person who has never had a problem with chemicals.

A common character defect is that of being critical of and debasing other people. This is invariably a desperate attempt by a person with low self-esteem to feel better by belittling others. This is a destructive trait because it does nothing to enhance one's character, and it often results in alienating others.

In recovery, people learn to take their *own* personality inventories and not other people's. We work on our *own* character defects, and try to make amends for the mistakes we have made. This generally results in our being less critical of others, as well as bringing about self-improvement. As our self-esteem improves with sobriety, there is no longer any *need* to belittle others in order to achieve a feeling of superiority.

Learn To Let Go of Guilt
❦

Should we feel guilty when things do not turn out well?

We often associate good and bad with success and failure, respectively. This may be appropriate in business, where the criterion of good or bad is the bottom line. If there is a profit, it was a good business venture. If there is a loss, it was a bad venture.

We often allow this kind of thinking to affect our moral judgments. We may feel guilty when we fail, even if what we did was ethically correct. This is a serious mistake, because no one is a prophet and we cannot foresee the future. All we can do is get the best advice and guidance possible, and be sincere in our intentions. Since we do not have control of how something will turn out, there is no reason to feel guilty if the result is unfavorable.

People in recovery have the advantage of being reminded that there are things over which we have no control, which we must turn over to a Higher Power. This should help prevent feelings of guilt that might otherwise occur when good intentions do not produce the desired results. It is only when people believe that everything is subject to our control that we may harbor unwarranted guilt feelings for unfavorable results.

Accept the Promise of Hope

Recovery may help cope with despair.

People who used chemicals may have experienced hallucinations, in which they saw or heard nonexistent objects and voices, or delusions, where they believed something that was not true.

People in recovery also learn that there are no grounds for despair or hopelessness. This is extremely important because, even in sobriety, depression with deep despair may occur, and we may feel hopeless when we do not see any way out.

It is difficult to convince people in a state of hopelessness that there is no reason for despair. We may not be able to conceive how things could ever change for the better, or how we could ever feel happy again. People who recover from chemicals, however, may remember that there were times whey they saw and heard things that just did not exist, and they realize that it is possible to misperceive. This can help them realize that, even if things appear hopeless, this too may be a misperception of depression, just as delusions or hallucinations are misperceptions brought on by chemical use. Therefore, they can accept the promise of hope.

Hopelessness leads to doing nothing, and this can sometimes bring about the very disaster that is feared. If we have hope, and continue to push on even through darkness, we can break through and eventually see the light of happiness.

From Denial to Self-Awareness

Denial is *not* the same as lying.

One doctor said, "When I told you last year that I was not using drugs, I was not lying. I was just not able to admit it to myself." Many people are not lying when they say they are not addicted. They are simply unable to see that they have lost control, or that there is any relationship between their chemical use and what is happening in their lives.

People who have overcome denial in regard to chemicals should realize that there is also denial of things other than chemicals. We may be unaware of being abrasive. We may avoid intimacy or relationships and not be aware of it. Someone who has succeeded in overcoming the denial of addiction should be aware how treacherous denial can be.

If our perceptions can be so misleading, can we ever be certain of anything? We can. First, we should take a careful inventory of ourselves and what it is that we think, feel, and believe. We should share our inventory with an objective observer, who may be able to point out our misperceptions. Since misperceptions are often rationalizations, whereby we defend ourselves from realizing that we have done something wrong, it helps if we decide never to defend a mistake, but rather to admit it promptly.

When denial is overcome, the correct perception of reality leads to better functioning and greater happiness.

Learn to Forgive Yourself
🍎

Just as we ask forgiveness from others, we must be able to forgive ourselves.

One woman wrote, "I *finally* am sober, and even enjoying it. I am definitely not a quick study. I vowed that I would someday let you know that all the help I received was not in vain. When I finished treatment, I was dry for a year and went to meetings, but that was all. I wouldn't talk to anybody. I never called my sponsor, because I didn't trust her.

"Although I felt better being dry, I was angry about being an alcoholic, and I didn't know how to live sober. I felt like I had a curse put on me. I would listen to people at meetings and I believed *they* had a disease, but that *I* was just a bad person. That was really sick and insane thinking.

"I couldn't shake it and I couldn't stand living with myself sober, so it was inevitable that I was going to drink again. I don't know why I got another chance. Many people never make it back. Why me? Well, why not me? Maybe I do deserve it after all.

"It's terrible not to be able to forgive yourself. While I did many things that I regret, I can't exactly pinpoint what it was that was so unforgivable. Why are we so hard on ourselves? Nobody ever really had to punish me, because I did the job so much better on myself than anyone else could."

The inability to forgive yourself can stand in the way of your recovery.

Sex, Addiction and Recovery

Sexual issues require special attention in recovery.

The sexual difficulties that arise as a consequence of addiction are often complex and may involve profound emotions. It is naïve to think that abstinence from chemicals will eliminate all difficulties in sexual relationships. During active addiction, both partners may be subjected to harsh words and abusive behavior. There may have been behavioral indiscretions that are not easily forgotten, that can leave deep wounds, and that can be removed only with reconstructive efforts over an extended period of time. Failure to respect each other's resentments and sensitivities may aggravate the problem.

Competent counseling is indispensable. There may be need for individual sessions to help each partner clarify feelings and eliminate distortions. There may also be need for joint sessions to facilitate an exchange of feelings and to avoid misinterpretations. It is important that the therapist have a thorough understanding of chemical dependency and the many factors that occur both during addiction and in recovery. Lack of such knowledge can result in the therapist's working at cross purposes with other recovery resources, and may cause confusion rather than bring resolution.

Don't Punish Yourself

Sick people are not bad people.

Jean's sponsor was not satisfied with her progress, although she was two years sober. One day Jean called me, and after a few minutes said, "I'm sorry I'm taking so much of your time. You have more important things to do."

"Like what?" I asked.

"You have to take care of your patients."

"Why is it more important that I talk with someone else rather than with you?" I asked.

"Oh, you know what I mean," Jean said. "I think it's wonderful that you've taken your time off for people like us. I mean like us dregs of humanity." Jean was convinced that because she was alcoholic she was a second-class citizen.

She did not accept that she had a disease, and continued to punish herself for being addicted.

People who realize that addiction is a disease can turn their attention to the business of getting better, but if they think of it as a moral weakness, they may become so preoccupied with guilt that they do not have the motivation or the energy to maximize their recovery.

People who have other types of diseases do not feel guilty or look for scapegoats. Rather, they try to become as healthy as possible. The same approach should be used with addiction.

Positive Thinking Brings Positive Results

❦

There is an aphorism, "Where there is a will there is a way."

At one treatment center, anytime someone says "I can't," the speaker must correct himself to say, "I don't *want* to do it."

Some things you want to do may not be realistic, because the sacrifice necessary to do them might be prohibitive and more than one could expect, in which case the "I can't" may be justified. But it is important to carefully analyze the statement "I can't do it," because it might really mean, "*I think* I can't," or "I *feel* I can't."

Some people hesitate to undertake something, or discontinue it because they feel they are unable to do it. This opinion is often erroneous. Underestimating your abilities and capacities is not at all uncommon. In fact, some people resort to chemicals because they feel unable to cope with stressful situations.

As people recover from addiction, they become increasingly aware of their abilities. They can then look back and see how unnecessary it was to escape into chemicals. This awareness of your abilities increases as sobriety progresses, so that with each additional increment of sobriety, the recovering person feels more efficient, more capable, and more likable.

The First Step Towards Recovery

One psychologist says, "Addiction is the inability of a person to reason effectively with himself and implement a decision for his own well being."

This definition refers to the *inability* to implement a decision, rather than an *unwillingness*, and avoids the fallacy that addiction is a lack of willpower.

This definition applies to more than chemical dependencies, including other self-destructive behaviors such as eating disorders, compulsive gambling, sexual addictions, and smoking. It can also include other self-defeating behaviors not considered to be addictive. It paves the way for applying what has been found to be effective in addictions to those self-defeating behaviors not characteristically addictive.

Before we can have effective treatment, we must make a correct diagnosis. In many self-defeating behaviors, the diagnosis should contain the word *inability* to implement a decision, which is really what is meant by the recognition that one is *powerless*. This is the first step in recovery from chemicals. Once the powerlessness is accepted, the other steps in recovery can follow.

The Twelve Steps of recovery enable you to build self-esteem and personality strength, so that you can truly master your own life, make proper decisions, and avoid self-defeating behavior.

Learning From a Crisis

A crisis can be a stimulus for growth.

One recovering person said, "I have been twelve years sober and working the Steps has certainly rebuilt my self-esteem. But there are still times when I doubt myself, and the old feelings of insecurity and fear of failure recur. Will I ever get rid of them?"

What I think happens can be demonstrated by folding a piece of cardboard, then unfolding and flattening it. Notice that the crease remains, and just a little pressure at this point will fold the cardboard again.

A recovering person can overcome a negative self-perception, but a trace may linger. Even years later, when you are confronted with stress or a challenge, that self-doubt and fear of failure may be resurrected, with a risk of relapse. But even if you do not go back to chemicals, the phenomenon known as a "dry drunk" can occur, with many of the behaviors characteristic of the active phase: depression, indecision, postponing, isolating, overcompensating, rationalizing, and projecting blame onto others.

Crises may occur even after a long sobriety. While these are risk points for relapse, they can also be take-off points for character growth. At these times, you should increase attendance at meetings, contact your sponsor, and renew your work on the Twelve Steps—just as though you were doing it for the first time. The growth that is achieved can be most gratifying.

Lectures Are Not the Answer

Extensive experience with alcohol can be useful in dealing with the recent increase in cocaine use.

Cutting off the supply of cocaine is unreliable. Alcoholics will tell you that when their wives hid the bottles or poured out the alcohol, it did not stop their drinking.

Showing young people the effects of cocaine does not work, either. How many people remember heading straight for the first bar after recovering from near fatal DTs? Many people have been threatened with loss of job, family, or driver's license, but threats do not work.

No one gets lectured as much as the alcoholic, and lectures are not the answer. People who recover remember the moment of truth—when they became aware of their powerlessness and their willingness to turn their lives over to a Higher Power. It was then that their *values* changed—and they changed, too. If we expect people to avoid cocaine, we have to help them achieve a sense of living and a quality of life that will make cocaine use unnecessary and undesirable.

The battle against cocaine is going to be a long and difficult one, and is going to require changes in the community, just as the family of the addict must change to participate in recovery. Our society must look not only at its habits of alcohol and drug use but also at its values for life. People who have recovered from alcoholism may be a great resource in defining these values.

Don't Get Tripped Up By "Maybe"
❦

Addicts are capable of some strange thinking.

One young man who entered treatment said that he had not considered himself addicted to cocaine because he was not a regular user. However, his wife was pressuring him to stop completely, and he decided that since he could go for weeks without using, he would just give it up completely. "After two weeks, I picked it up again. That proved it to me," he said. "I became convinced that it was absolutely impossible for me to stop on my own maybe."

This is an example of the contradictory thinking that can occur in addiction. This man said that it was now *absolutely impossible* for him to stop on his own, *maybe*. Absolutely impossible—maybe. Aren't these diametrically opposed? Of course! Then how can both be in the same sentence? That is how people think in addiction.

This same kind of thinking may also occur with the Third Step. We become ready to turn our entire lives over to the will of God, *maybe*. We may *think* we are turning things over, but a closer analysis shows that we are still holding on, as if we can turn things over with the reservation that we can take them back if we wish to.

This contradictory thinking is something we need to recheck in sobriety. It may be the prelude to relapse, when all our absolute convictions end up with "maybe."

The Serenity Prayer
🍂

The Serenity Prayer is indeed a pillar of recovery.

One recovering person asked, "Why is it called the Serenity Prayer? After all, there are three parts to it: the *serenity* to accept that which we cannot change, the *courage* to change that which we can, and the *wisdom* to know the difference. Why is it never referred to as the 'courage' prayer or the 'wisdom' prayer?"

This is more than just semantics. As difficult as it may be to accept some things in life, it is nevertheless easier to accept things than to try to change them. Too often we are afraid to change, perhaps because we lack the confidence to do so. We resign ourselves to some changeable situations, accepting them as unchangeable.

Of course, that is why we pray for the wisdom to know the difference, to be shown which things are changeable. But we need to remember that the answer to our prayers usually does not come in revelations, as in a prophetic dream. The answers to prayers often come through people, because God frequently uses people as instruments to convey the answers we seek. When our sponsors or counselors tell us to do something, and they assure us that we are able to accomplish it, that may be how the wisdom to know the difference is being suggested to us.

Maybe we should alternate: call it the Serenity Prayer one month, the Courage Prayer the next, and the Wisdom Prayer the next. All three components should be given equal emphasis.

The Program is Versatile

The Twelve Step program of recovery is indeed a divine gift to humankind.

Although it began as a program for recovery from alcoholism, its benefits became evident for other problems that threaten people's survival. We find the Twelve Steps being used for drug addiction (NA), compulsive gambling (GA), eating disorders (OA), and codependency (Al-Anon and Nar-Anon).

Those who found the miracle of their recovery in AA may feel that AA is the answer to every problem, and that if they have another problem, AA should be able to handle it also.

A food processor has several attachments. The same motor can be used for different purposes, provided you use the right attachment. If you wish to bake a cake, you use the beater attachment; to grind meat or nuts, you use the grinder; to slice or shred vegetables, you use the slicer or the shredder. If you want to slice, but you attach the grinder, you're not going to get the desired result.

The Twelve Step program is the motor that propels recovery, but it does require the proper attachments. If in addition to a drinking problem you have a gambling problem, you must use the GA attachment. For an eating disorder, you must use the OA attachment. If you are involved with a family member who has a problem, you must use the Al-Anon or Nar-Anon attachment.

Going to another of the Twelve Step programs should not affect your original program. It can only enrich it.

Be Fair to Yourself
❦

Sometimes we do not put constructive techniques to use. For example, when children bring home a test or homework with an A+, we might display these on the refrigerator. This not only tells our children that we are proud of their achievement but also reminds them of their capacity to produce excellence.

If they bring home a test with a failing grade, we never put that one on the refrigerator. We never tell them, "Look how terrible you are," or remind them of their failure every time they go to the refrigerator.

Why don't we use this logic on ourselves? Why do we wallow in the misery of our mistakes and see ourselves as failures? Some of us never let go of the past. Yet when we succeed, we dismiss that as a freak accident.

Recognizing our successes and being aware of our potential need not result in conceit or vanity. Even if we are aware that we have superior skills, that does not mean that we are "better" than someone else. If other people had been equally endowed, they might have performed even better.

The way to deal with our failures is the way we deal with our children when they fail a test. We try to see why we failed and how to do better next time, all the while keeping our attitude positive.

We should learn from our mistakes, but not dwell on them.

The Culture of Instant Gratification
🍎

Compared to years ago, there is probably much wider use of alcohol and drugs today.

Why are many intelligent people not discouraged from using chemicals by their very obvious and harmful consequences? Studies have shown that when young people are shown films about the disastrous consequences of drug abuse, their use actually *increases*. They seem to see only the mystique and euphoria of chemical use; they block out all the horrible consequences. Perhaps some of the ideas that are the basis for today's life-style may imperceptively influence people's use of chemicals.

Much of our economy is dependent on a "buy now, pay later" attitude. What would happen if we did not have credit cards? Would we really buy as much if we had to pay cash for everything? Most major purchases—such as automobiles, furniture, and appliances—are bought on credit. We pay dearly for credit in terms of high interest rates, but that seems acceptable. We get whatever we desire, even if, in the long run, we must pay much more than the purchase price. Some families have gone bankrupt by spending more than they earn.

The buy now, pay later attitude may be contributing to the rise in chemical abuse. How can we convince our children to forgo the high of chemicals because of future harmful effects, when our life-style tells them it's okay to get what you want *now*, even though you may have to pay an exorbitant price later on?

Learn to Relax
❦

Relaxation is not always easy.

I use self-hypnosis to relax. I allow my mind to drift to a pleasant past event; invariably, I relive some childhood experiences when we had a cabin near a lake. In my trance I swim, fish, and hike—all the fun things of the past.

Why I have to go into the past to relax? Why can I not relax in the present? Why is relaxation in the past so much better?

The answer is that, as with any pleasant event of the past, we know how it turned out. Whether it was a picnic, hike, or ball game, we know the day ended up being enjoyable. Reliving the experience is relaxing because we know the ending. In the present, there is no certainty how the day will turn out. Too many things could happen to spoil our relaxation.

A lack of relaxation may be related to uncertainty. We may be unable to enjoy the present because of a fear that the good things might not last. It is only when the successful present becomes the past that we can enjoy it.

But if we are able to turn our lives over to God, and develop the kind of trust that allows us to say, "My life is in Your hands, and You know best," much of our anxiety will be gone and we can enjoy the healthy, chemical-free relaxation we all need.

Twelve Step Meetings: They Work
❦

Many Twelve Step meetings close with: "Keep coming back, it works."

Some people are reluctant to admit they have an addiction. They seek psychiatric treatment rather than join an addiction recovery program because they might then be fortunate enough to be diagnosed as having something other than addiction, perhaps a neurosis or even a psychosis—*anything*, as long as it's not addiction.

The various kinds of psychotherapy that are not addiction oriented get people to think things out and analyze why and how things got to be this way—why they have certain feelings, and so on. But experience has shown that analyzing the past does not have much effect on addiction. Psychology and psychiatry have abundant theories, while the Twelve Step program does not use much theory. It has only one redeeming feature: it works.

How many people who take aspirin know why it relieves pain? Even most doctors don't understand why aspirin helps pain. Why take it or prescribe it? Because *it works*.

The reason water puts out fire is because it prevents oxygen from reaching the flames, but if your house were afire, you would not want a firefighter to theorize. You would want someone to pour on the water because "it works."

This is the message of recovery. Don't theorize; just keep coming back, because it works.

Learn to Think in New Ways
❦

Many problems do have solutions.

Addicts sometimes have an "either-or" type of thinking. They may be very rigid, seeing things in extremes, without the flexibility that exists in reality.

One addict was in a quandary whether to go back with his wife or terminate the marriage. He was frustrated because neither option was good. Someone suggested he try a temporary separation and that, while working on his recovery, his wife could avail herself of counseling and join Al-Anon. Over a period of time, they could look at the viability of their marriage. It was evident from this man's reaction that this possibility had not occurred to him.

Whether it is with a marriage, a job, or a relationship, thinking only in extremes is destructive.

Changing your way of thinking is not easy. You may have been using either-or thinking even before active chemical use began.

We must be patient while thought processes are transformed. The family as well as the addicted person needs to understand that changes in thought habits are gradual. Improvements in thinking and behavior do occur, however, and when thinking only in extremes is discarded, solutions to problems can be found.

The Meaning of Life

What does life really consist of?

Some people may have a distorted perception of what there is to life. They think that there must be more to life than they are experiencing. Many addicts feel cheated because they are not getting out of life what other people seem to.

One recovering person said, "My whole world was drab and gray. My wife was gray, the children were gray, the job was gray, my car was gray, everything was gray! I can't stand a gray world. I need color! When I drank, alcohol made the world colorful."

Some people use chemicals to get *high*, but others say they need chemicals just to feel normal. The idea that there are more thrills to life than you are getting is a fantasy. You feel whatever everyone else feels, but maybe it just doesn't measure up to what you *think* you should be feeling.

Sometimes there is an inability to feel. The chemically dependent person has shut down the feeling system in order to avoid all unpleasant feelings. If this is your case, you need help in learning to deal with feelings, and to dismantle the blockade that prevents you from feeling joy and excitement.

There may not be a paradise on earth, but life can be interesting and even enjoyable. If we don't see it that way, we need some help to correct our perceptions.

Spirituality in Recovery
❦

There is a spiritual component to recovery.

Why are addictive diseases unique to human beings? Why are wild animals not addicted to food, sex, or intoxicating plants? Animals seem to have an effective cap on their desires. When the biological function of a drive is fulfilled, they stop.

We may not recognize that our discontent is due to a lack of spirituality. We try to overcome our discontent with something that has worked with other feelings of discontent—food, drugs, alcohol, sex, or money. But these give only transitory gratification. Since they cannot satisfy our spiritual cravings, we remain as miserable as ever, and indulge more and more in a futile attempt to feel better.

Some people give up chemicals, but they become compulsive gamblers or overeaters. This is just another futile attempt to satisfy the craving for spirituality.

Many recovering people say, "During periods of abstinence, I would feel a terrible void inside myself. Now I know that that void was the space where God belonged."

Addiction is, among other things, a spiritual disease. True sobriety cannot be achieved unless that specific need is satisfied.

Stay With the Program
❦

Addiction can be arrested, but not cured.

The disease process of addiction continues even if we are abstinent. Many people have relapsed after years of abstinence, finding that the physical and emotional effects of the chemical were as though they had never stopped.

The Twelve Steps is a treatment program for addiction, and treatment can be stopped only when the disease is cured. Since the disease continues even during abstinence, there is never a time when treatment can be discontinued.

People who stop working the program are apt to develop behavioral symptoms. Leaving the program can be a statement of "I don't need any help," which may be a reassertion of omnipotence. Personality changes may recur: hanging onto resentments, self-righteousness, spending too much time at work and alienating the family, avoiding religion, blaming everyone for whatever goes wrong, and perhaps most of all, trying to control everything and everyone. Even if this does not lead to chemical relapse, it makes everyone miserable and may result in job loss, marriage breakup, alienation, and loneliness.

The Twelve Step program is a treatment for a faulty life-style. As long as the disease is present, you should continue the treatment.

Overcoming "Morbid Expectations"
❧

Good things can persist.

A young man who was just several days away from his first anniversary of sobriety was admitted with a drinking relapse. Very tearfully he said, "I knew something had to happen. Nothing in my life has ever been consistently good. This time I was feeling so good. For the first time my wife told me she loved me, and I even got a promotion at work. I knew it couldn't last and that something catastrophic had to happen. Every time the phone rang I knew it was a message that my child had been struck by a car. I couldn't take the suspense any more, so I drank to get it over with."

This is the phenomenon of "morbid expectations." Many people have a feeling of being jinxed. Or perhaps they have failed so often in the past that they feel more comfortable with failure. As painful as failure is, at least it is familiar. Success is something new, something unknown, and the unknown can be frightening.

Therapy can help overcome the irrational feeling of being jinxed. A sponsor can help with the fear of the unknown that accompanies success. If we develop a trust in a Higher Power, and believe that God looks out for us, we can overcome the anxiety and tension of morbid expectations.

While unpleasant occurrences may occur in life, there is no reason to anticipate them.

Finding Real Love

Not all that goes for love is really love.

One young woman with a history of chemical relapses had a pattern of romantic disappointments. I advised her, "Be careful of getting into relationships where you think the person loves you, when in reality he loves himself. At this point in your recovery you cannot tell the difference, and you are vulnerable to exploitation. When you discover you have been exploited, you become angry and bitter, and then you relapse."

"I do that every time," the woman responded.

We often misinterpret love. A man can "love" his wife and children, and he can "love" spaghetti. But when we love a food, we actually love ourselves, and the tasty food just provides the gratification of our desire.

We can love people in the same way. A man may love a woman because she satisfies his needs. He really then loves himself, and the woman is just a vehicle for providing gratification.

True love is not self-centered. It exists when we are ready to sacrifice our convenience and pleasures for the well-being and happiness of another person.

The True Path to Recovery

There is a proven method to recovery.

Suppose you were in a maze, where only one of the paths leads to the goal. How can you possibly find the right path?

One way is to pick a path and follow it. If it ends up in a dead end, retrace your steps and mark the entrance so you know not to try that one again. Repeat this until you finally locate the right path. You may exhaust yourself in the process.

Suppose, however, that someone who has already found the correct path, and is standing on a high platform, calls out to you, "No! Don't take that path, it goes nowhere. Follow my instructions, and I will direct you to the right one." It would be foolish to ignore this advice and proceed with the trial-and-error method.

Recovery from chemical dependency is much like a complicated maze. Many people have tried various methods, all in vain. A person who fails to achieve sobriety may not even mark the wrong path, and repeat the same mistake many times. Even if you tried a new method each time, there is a limit to how much abuse the body can take. By the time you discover the right path, it may be too late.

There are people who have discovered how to achieve sobriety. They can tell us which ways are ineffective and which ways work. It is most foolish to reject the proven wisdom of experience.

Overcome Distorted Thinking
❦

Addictive thinking can be very strange.

Addicts may think they are being logical, and cannot understand why others do not see things their way. Other people may fall prey to this illogical kind of thinking.

A young woman grew increasingly addicted to prescription drugs, and became dysfunctional. Yet she thought that she was unable to afford treatment because of inadequate insurance coverage.

I told the woman that there was a fund available that provided interest-free loans, which she could repay with the money she would save by discontinuing drugs. The woman said that this was impossible, because she would not disclose her expenditure to her husband "in order to protect him."

This woman sincerely believed she was being kind to her husband. She considered it a kindness that she not avail herself of the loan in order to overcome her problem. She could not see that remaining addicted, dysfunctional, and spending $400 a month on drugs was far from a kindness.

This distorted addictive thinking may not disappear even with the onset of abstinence. We need the help of competent therapists and people with long sobriety to help us avoid the pitfalls of faulty judgments made early in recovery.

Gratitude

People may have difficulty accepting gratitude from others.

Sometimes we thank a person for something, and the response is, "Don't mention it." People may want to minimize what they've done. However, "Don't mention it" may also be taken as a rejection of gratitude. It's like someone's refusing to accept a gift, which is not a pleasant feeling. It would be better to say, "I'm glad I could be of help."

When a person does not express gratitude immediately, we may wonder, "Doesn't he appreciate what I did for him?" and we may build up resentment. When this person finally does express gratitude, we may then respond with a mixture of acknowledgment and resentment for the delay.

When someone excuses himself for not having thanked you earlier, you might say, "I never doubted your appreciation. I understand that can happen. It has happened to me more than once." You will thus be both considerate and truthful.

Time Takes Time

Time takes time.

One recovering woman wrote: "It was four years ago this month that I was taken into your office, utterly beaten, wanting to die, but did not have the courage to take my own life, so sick both mentally and spiritually. It was thanks to you that I went back to AA and that I made it through those first two years.

"Looking back I can see how sick I was and thought I was doing just fine. The only thing I did right during those first two years was not drink and go to meetings.

"I want you to know that it has taken me four years to feel good about myself, to feel that I have something to offer other people. I don't have to keep tearing myself down, and I don't have to keep myself sick anymore. Words can't express how I feel. I'm just so grateful to my God, the program, and the people."

Although this woman did not perceive any changes in the first two years, she did attend meetings and did not drink. Her perception is that it took four years for her to overcome her unwarranted negative feelings. Four years is indeed a long time, but some things cannot be hurried. It is unrealistic to expect feelings of inadequacy that you've held for decades to disappear in just a few months.

This young woman's message emphasizes that "time takes time." We must have patience in recovery.

Learn to Ask For Help
❧

There is a time when accepting gifts is appropriate.

In the letter quoted yesterday, the recovering young woman continues: "You'll be glad to know that I swallowed my pride and gave my dad a chance to be a parent and a father. I asked him to help me buy a new car. I got a new car in November, my first real car with a heater that worked, air-conditioning, and a trunk. That car means so much to me because it is the symbol of my recovery. I believe that Dad and Mom were pleased that I finally asked for their help."

During active addiction there may be "enabling" that is destructive, and loving parents may have to reluctantly withhold things from their children. When this woman recovered, it was then appropriate for her parents to help her. Because she had felt undeserving, she had refused their help earlier, which certainly must have frustrated them. As she developed better self-esteem in recovery, she was able to accept her parents' gifts, much to their joy as well as to her own advantage.

Constructive help during recovery should not be rejected. There is no need to be deprived unnecessarily.

The Lessons of Recovery

There is a message in recovery.

Children who grew up with an addicted parent sometimes develop character traits that cause problems in adjusting to life, even if the parent has long since recovered.

One of the strengths of the recovery program is that it does not avoid uncomfortable aspects of reality. During addiction we make believe that the harsh parts of life don't exist. In recovery we learn to deal even with unpleasant things. If our past behavior adversely affected the people we love, we must deal with that. If we can do something to rectify our mistakes, we must sincerely offer to do so, and not assume that a verbal apology is enough. But we can do only what we can do. If we cannot undo the past, we must be able to accept it.

We should also remember that recovering addicts send a powerful message to their children—one of courage to overcome the ravages of addiction. Recovery provides a living example not to give up when everything looks bleak. Life can be difficult even in the absence of addiction. But if a child learns that there is no giving up, that with hope, trust, and faith there is a chance for happiness, this is a valuable lesson.

Don't Set Yourself Up For Failure
🍎

We may make self-fulfilling prophecies.

Some people "set themselves up," and manipulate their environment in such a way that the results are predictable.

A person involved in a business venture or a personal relationship may believe she will fail. She may feel she will be blamed for the failure and accused of being inadequate. In order to avoid being blamed, she involves someone else in such a way that, if she fails, the other person will get the blame. But in the process she brings about the failure she feared. Thus, she sets herself up for failure.

Or suppose you want something very much, but don't feel capable of achieving it. Because you lack the confidence to get what you desire, you put someone else up to the task of getting it; you depend on others for things you should do yourself. Then, when other people have their own priorities and do not do your bidding, you do not see this disappointment as your doing but, rather, due to other people's lack of consideration.

Recovering people sometimes set themselves up so they can blame others when disappointments come. They fail to see that they designed things to result in failure. But by consistently working on the recovery program, and with good sponsorship and competent counseling, you can prevent setting yourself up for failure.

How to Take a Compliment
❦

Why should a pleasant comment be rejected?

A young woman entered treatment in a debilitated state. When her appearance significantly improved, I said to her, "Agnes, you're really beginning to look good." She responded with an obscenity. She later apologized, explaining, "You said something positive to me, and I don't know how to handle that. I only know how to handle negative comments. I get those all the time."

Addicts may be irritated by complimentary remarks, and therefore behave in a manner that elicits negative comments. Which comes first—chemical use or the inability to accept positive comments? By the time the individual is deep into addiction, there have been so many turns of the cycle that it is impossible to resolve this "chicken or egg" dilemma.

It is not really important that we know which came first. What is important is that we recognize how eliciting negativity has become an established pattern, and how recovery can result in positive comments.

People in early recovery may avoid contact with those who make complimentary remarks, and may thus lose the support of the people they need the most. Bear this in mind when relating to people in early recovery, as well as while you are recovering yourself. Change can be a problem, even when it is a change for the better. During that period of adaptation, patience on everyone's part is essential.

Live in the Present

The true challenge in life is the present.

Many people think it would be wonderful to foretell the future. If we knew today which stocks would go up tomorrow, what a profit we could make!

But perhaps foreknowledge is not all that useful. Almost every alcoholic I know has been remorseful following drinking, and has vowed never to drink again. But when they drink again, they know what is going to happen, but do it anyway. Sometimes a person may think "This time will be different," but there are times when the alcoholic does not deceive himself, and drinks in spite of the consequences. Foreknowledge doesn't always help. If an alcoholic knew which stocks were going to go up, he might find some rationalization for not buying them.

A wise man is greater than a prophet. A prophet can see the future, but a wise man can see the present.

Preoccupation with the future is an escape from the present. We can make plans and resolutions, and fantasize to our heart's content. If any sacrifices are necessary in the future, it is so easy to deal with them now. That's what "I'll quit tomorrow" is all about.

It is the difficult *present* that requires so much effort. The demands of the present are real, and any sacrifices must be made now.

The program reminds us that we must deal with today—the only day we can really do something about.

Setback or Opportunity?

❧

A wise man once said, "Whenever you fall, try to pick something up."

When we stand upright, our vision is focused at eye level. Valuable things may be lying in the mud, where no one can appreciate their beauty. Furthermore, they may be damaged when people inadvertently step on them. But if you look around at ground level, you may see things to which you would have otherwise been oblivious.

Not every fall should be adjudged to be clumsiness. A fall may be God's way of bringing our heads and eyes down to ground level. The most common reaction to a fall is to utter an expression of anger, get up, and brush oneself off. This may be a missed opportunity.

People can have numerous kinds of falls: a broken relationship, a business failure, illness, disappointment, a slip in sobriety. When we experience distress, is it not comforting when someone empathizes with us? Who can empathize as sincerely as someone who has experienced a similar adversity? Keep this in mind when you experience any kind of adversity, and do not be so preoccupied with your own bitterness that you miss the opportunity to identify with others. Of course you must get up and continue on your way. But before you do so, be sure to look around. The fall may have had a purpose: there may be someone whom you can now help.

Pray Every Day
❦

Each day we ask for another day of sobriety.

There is a rather enigmatic verse in the Book of Proverbs, which states, "All the days of the poor are wretched, but if he has a good heart, his meal is always festive."

How can our meals be festive if we are wretched? The answer is that the person who must struggle for a day's subsistence is not necessarily wretched. She may appear so to others, but because she must look to God for her daily bread, she is a constant beneficiary of God's bounty. She is God's personal guest each day.

In the biblical account of the Garden of Eden, God cursed the serpent that he would eat earth all the days of his life. Why is it a curse to always have food readily available? All living things look to God and pray in their own way for daily subsistence. But God was so angry with the serpent that He said, "You can have your food always in front of you, and never be lacking for anything. Don't pray to me! You are so despicable that I don't even wish to hear your voice."

When our existence depends upon praying for each day of sobriety, it is the highest compliment we can receive. If we must call upon God every day, that means He wishes to hear us every day. Being in a program that teaches us to live one day at a time, and that we are dependent upon God every day, is indeed a blessing.

Find Your Inner Voice
❦

Recovery involves avoiding what we *want* to do and doing what we are supposed to do.

Some say that in recovery we should be guided by our "inner voice." This may sound good, but what about the inner voice that used to say, "Go ahead and take a drink; you need it just to settle your nerves. One drink won't hurt you." How are we to distinguish between this destructive voice and the wise inner voice?

The difference may be a subtle one, but with a little analysis, it is possible to distinguish between the two voices. How does the tightrope artist keep his balance walking across a wire? The trick in walking a tightrope is that when you feel a tug toward one side, lean just a bit to the opposite side, and that way you keep your equilibrium.

There is a definite difference between an inner voice and an urge. An urge is when you feel a tug, that you are being drawn to something—not at all like an inner voice. The inner voice tells you what you *should* do, and is not an urge. The urge is to take just one drink or just one hit of cocaine. The inner voice says, "Don't be stupid. Every time you've done that in the past it was disastrous."

The urge is your addiction talking to you. The way to *overcome* the urge is to hear the message of the inner voice.

The Miracle of Recovery
❧

Sobriety is indeed a miracle.

Some people see the greatest miracle in the recovering person—someone who had lost everything, and who had hit rock bottom. However, when a person has been totally devastated by chemicals, it is literally a choice between life and death. And since there is a natural fear of death, it is not all that surprising that this person chooses sobriety. What *is* remarkable is the person who recovers *before* reaching bottom.

It is remarkable that people can give up alcohol or drugs when these chemicals have been the only thing that made life tolerable for them. When people join the Twelve Step fellowship, they meet people for whom life without chemicals is not only tolerable but actually enjoyable, and they trust these people. This is so special because addicts often lack even the rudiments of trust. The fact that they have sufficient trust in someone to be willing to give up chemicals is nothing less than miraculous.

When we work with people who are in early recovery, we are asking them to trust us and accept our assurance that life without chemicals is livable. We must behave in a manner to deserve that trust. This not only helps *them* but also makes *us* better people.

Celebrating Sobriety

One recovering person celebrated his seventeenth anniversary by taking a trip to the Holy Land. He wrote:

"As I pen this note to you, the dawn breaks here on the shore of Galilee. The rising sun burns through the morning mist and all is still except for the doves and an occasional fish splashing in the quiet waters. I am at peace with myself.

"How different it is from that morning seventeen years ago when the sun rose on what I hoped would be the last painful day of my life.

"My life, then devoid of hope, was forever changed and filled with the primeval expectancy of life giving birth to life. Since that day it has been my special privilege to stand on the path of many headed into the gates of insanity and hell, and show a sign that they need not go this way, but with the radiance of God's love to their back, turn and walk with God's will to a new life. Today is another day of celebration as I reflect on God's will for me and pray for the power to carry it out.

"Seventeen years ago I was deeply in debt. I lost my home and we faced bankruptcy. We elected to repay the debt, and so began years of debt reduction which finally ended this year. I am free at last, sober and filled with the joy of life."

Paranoia

Sometimes we misinterpret other people's actions.

Suppose you walk into a room full of people, and as you enter someone walks out. What does that mean? Absolutely nothing. He may be leaving the room to make a phone call. But you may think, "He is leaving the room because he saw me coming. He does not like me." That sounds somewhat paranoid.

Although we may not become actually paranoid, sometimes we do interpret things wrongly when we relate everything to ourselves. We may be so self-conscious, so sensitive, and perhaps so expecting of criticism or rejection that we read intentions into other people's behavior.

How many times have you discovered that people were offended by something you said, when in fact you did not have the slightest intention of offending them? Give others the same consideration we give ourselves: do not impute unfriendly motives to other people's behavior.

Because our thinking may be skewed by feelings that are groundless, we would be wise to check our interpretations with someone else. We might then realize that we have created monsters where none exist. We can rid ourselves of unnecessary misery, and also remove obstacles that can undermine friendly relationships.

Learning to Pray
🍎

Prayer is an important component of recovery.

We begin each day by praying for another day of sobriety, and ask God for serenity, courage, and wisdom.

Some people, especially early in recovery, complain that they do not know how to pray. "I have tried to pray," they say, "but I can't seem to get the hang of it." Some veterans in the program recommend, "Just say the words even if you don't have the feeling. The feeling will come eventually."

Sometimes the hindrance to prayer stems from a fierce self-sufficiency. We simply cannot get ourselves to ask for help from anyone, even God, because we must do everything ourselves. Such feelings of omnipotence are characteristic of active addiction, and should dissipate in recovery.

We generally pray for what we feel are the necessities of life: health, wisdom, and the means to live comfortably. But prayer is as much a necessity of life as those other things. Why not pray for the ability to pray? We might say, "Dear God, I've been trying to communicate to You, but I just don't know how. Please help me reach You. Please help me pray."

This is not all that strange. We take appetizers before a meal. If we can eat in order to stimulate our desire to eat, then we can also pray in order to stimulate our desire to pray.

The Dangers of Codependency

People may become victims when they try to be saviors.

It is simply a matter of time and energy. If we use up a great deal of time trying to save others, we will have little time for ourselves. If we expend our energy on others, we'll be exhausted when it comes to our own needs.

You might ask, "Is it not right to be selfless, and place other people's interests before our own?"

In an airplane, the flight attendant instructs: "In case of a loss in cabin pressure, oxygen masks will appear before you. If you are traveling with a child, put your own mask on first, and then attend to the child." If you try to help the child while you are short of breath, you might get things so messed up that neither of you gets any oxygen. Thus, if we wish to help others, we must meet our own essential needs first.

People who are codependent often violate this rule. They believe that by self-sacrifice and catering to the addictive behavior they are helping that person. The fact is that codependents not only become victims but enable and prolong the addiction rather than help stop it.

Anyone who deals with a chemically dependent person, whether it be a spouse, family member, close friend, or employer, should avail himself of an outside opinion, such as an addiction counselor or an Al-Anon or Nar-Anon group. Otherwise, the entire family may be adversely affected by wrong things done with the best of intentions.

Learn to Let Go
🍎

True love is reciprocated.

There is a verse in the Book of Proverbs that reads, "Just as water reflects an image, that is how a person reflects another person's feelings." In other words, feelings are never one-way. The way you feel toward another person is very similar to how that person feels toward you.

Sometimes one partner in a relationship rejects the other, but the other fights vigorously to keep the relationship going. A wife may say that she no longer wishes to be married to this man, yet he desperately tries to preserve the marriage, protesting his intense love for her. Isn't this an example of a one-way love?

The answer is that there are things that resemble love but are not true love—anymore than fool's gold is real gold. What the rejected partner may feel is the pain of rejection, and he wishes to hold on because he cannot tolerate being rejected. This is a self-love rather than love for the other person.

This breakup may happen in the relationship of an addict. If someone really wants out of the relationship, it is foolish to preserve it. Do not be fooled into thinking that you love the other person so intensely that you cannot live without him or her. True love is reciprocated. If it is not true love, why try to preserve the relationship?

Self-Awareness vs. Self-Deception

The Twelve Steps are in proper sequence.

One man complained that he relapsed in spite of working a diligent AA program. Analysis revealed he was really not doing so.

On approaching the Third Step, he was willing to turn his life over to the care of God but, because his life had become quite debased during his drinking years, he did not think it respectful to turn such a contaminated life over to God. He felt he must first get everything in proper order, and only then would it be appropriate to turn his life over to God: a shiny new life, worthy of God's attention. He was going to delay the Third Step until after he completed the Ninth Step.

Much of addiction deals with a delusion of omnipotence. If we can get our act together by ourselves, we will have little need for God. This man deceived himself. Although he admitted he was powerless, that his life had become unmanageable, and that only a power greater than himself could restore his sanity, he still believed he was in control. He felt he could get everything in perfect order by himself *before* turning his life over to God. He thought he was working the AA program, but he was really working his *own* program.

Avoid such mistakes. Take advantage of the wisdom of people with long sobriety, for whom the program has worked well. They can help with self-deception.

The Challenge of Self-Discovery

Self-discovery can be a challenge.

The requirement of the Fourth Step to "Make a *fear-less* moral inventory" indicates that there is something frightening about this step. Most people say that a careful self-examination reveals many of their character defects, and this is frightening. However, many people entering recovery are aware of all the mistakes they have made and of their character defects, so none of this would come as a surprise.

It is not the discovery of our defects that is frightening, but the discovery of our strengths and skills. We discover how much good there is in us and how capable we really are.

You ask, "Why is there a need to be fearless in discovering one's strengths and capabilities?" The answer is that being aware of our potential imposes the responsibility of accomplishing things. If we fear failure, we find it easy to think, "There's no use in my trying. I can't do it anyway." Remaining in a rut may be comfortable, while getting out of the rut is frightening. So we need to muster all the courage we can to face discovering how good we really are, and that we have strengths and abilities we never dreamt of before.

Don't be afraid to discover the good within yourself. You will ultimately enjoy it.

Even Legal Drugs Are Treacherous
❦

All mood-altering drugs are potentially addictive.

Even drugs prescribed by doctors can be addictive. Relatively few medical schools provide adequate information about addiction. Therefore many otherwise excellent physicians may be unaware of the addictive qualities of some drugs.

The pharamaceutical industry aggressively promotes its products. Just a few years ago there were full-page ads in medical journals praising the sedative Quaalude, a drug which soon after had to be taken off the market because of its lethal addictive action.

People who have discontinued regular use of tranquilizers report both physical and emotional withdrawal symptoms lasting up to two years—far longer than the withdrawal symptoms of even cocaine and heroin.

Anyone with a history of addiction should be wary of potentially addictive drugs. If they are medically necessary, consult an expert on addiction. Even people without an addictive history should be cautious about using potentially addictive drugs for more than a short period of time.

Addictive drugs are treacherous. Preventing addiction is far superior to curing it.

Impatience Can Be Dangerous
❦

Don't dismiss the slogan "Time takes time" as silly.

The modern world operates with unprecedented pressure for immediate results. In a matter of just a few decades, modern technology has revolutionized the means of communication and travel. We have become accustomed to expecting things to happen fast, and the faster the better.

Our kitchens are equipped with instant foods and microwave ovens. Our television sets may be "instant on" models, eliminating the twenty-second warmup. Long-distance telephone companies compete to connect your call faster, while fax machines transmit documents around the world with practically the speed of light. Except for pregnancy, virtually everything has been speeded up.

The greatest threat to sobriety is impatience. We are vulnerable to frustration when things don't happen when we want them to. During active addiction, we can measure tolerance of delay with a stopwatch; the fact that chemicals have such rapid action characterizes addiction.

It is a challenge to learn to delay in a culture that thrives on high speed. We must be reminded that "time takes time," and beware that everyone else's preoccupation with instant results should not affect our own lives.

Women In Recovery

Women's issues in addiction require special attention.

When treatment programs began to proliferate, the initial therapists were primarily people who had recovered from alcoholism. There was a predominance of men, just as there was among people who entered the treatment centers. Consequently, the treatment techniques developed were male oriented. The occasional woman patient who entered treatment received a program designed for men.

Addiction is different in men and women. There are some physical differences in chemical action, and some great differences in psychological effects. In addition, women suffer a double standard, whereby an alcoholic man is thought of as "just having had too much of a good thing," whereas a woman alcoholic is apt to be judged morally degenerate. People may not consider a male alcoholic to be a failure as a father, but a woman alcoholic is automatically considered a failure as a mother.

Such attitudes not only result in a greater denial of addiction among women and a greater coverup by the family, but also cause much lower self-esteem.

Addiction is a disease that does not discriminate. Women must receive the same consideration as men; furthermore, their unique emotional problems require special attention (see next message).

New Pressures on Women

There are indeed special emotional issues faced by addicted women.

The social status of women has undergone recent changes, with greater numbers of women entering business management and the professions. Since this is a new phenomenon, many women in these new roles may not have had appropriate preparation. They may have been raised to believe that women are supposed to be housewives or teachers (both maternal roles), or nurses or secretaries. If they entered a field in which they are required to be assertive or aggressive, they may feel awkward and under great stress.

Because of the novelty of women in these positions, they may have required, or held themselves to, more exacting standards of performance. Things readily forgiven if done by men are not so easily overlooked when done by women.

To deal with these stresses of modern life, or perhaps to avoid showing signs of stress (which might be interpreted as their being inappropriate for these new roles), some women have sought the tranquilizing effects of chemicals.

The recovering woman should be aware of these societal stresses, and find constructive ways of managing them (see next message).

Childhood Sexual Abuse

Special attention may be needed to overcome the effects of childhood sexual abuse.

Some addicted women were victims of early sexual abuse. Their recovery may be hindered by the difficulty in dealing with these extremely painful emotions. The memories may be totally repressed or even when remembered, may not be shared in therapy.

Although adult women understand that they were helpless when they were abused in childhood, this does not eradicate the feelings of shame they may bear, because emotions are not always subject to logic. The low self-esteem that begins in childhood consequent to such trauma persists into adulthood, and may be a major component of later negative feelings about herself that can complicate and fuel the addiction. Anger, resentment, and profound distress that result from childhood molestation may add to the already heavy burden these women carry.

Society tends to blame the victim, and sometimes we blame ourselves as well. These issues may be so sensitive that they cannot be shared at meetings, but they should be alleviated in counseling. They can also be dealt with in the privacy of the relationship to *God as we understand Him*, in the firm knowledge that He understands us.

Spirituality, Humanity and Freedom

Just what is spirituality?

Biology teaches that human beings are *Homo sapiens*, or baboons with intellect.

The real difference, however is that animals are driven totally by their internal drives. If an animal is hungry or thirsty, it must look for food or water. Animals cannot make a conscious decision to abstain from anything. They are slaves to their internal drives.

Humans have the capacity to abstain from any drive, however. They can be masters of their urges and passions; they do not need to be enslaved by them. This capacity to be master over oneself, rather than a slave to one's passions, is the human "spirit." Exercising that capacity is *spirituality*.

Nowhere is people's enslavement as absolute as in addiction. A person who is driven to use chemicals has no choice. To the degree that we lose freedom, we lose our humanity.

But recovery restores freedom. We can choose whether or not to drink or use chemicals, and to exercise the power of the spirit to master our urges. This is what an animal cannot do.

Spirituality, humanity, and freedom are identical. When we become more free, we also become more spiritual and more fully human.

The Insanity of Modern Society
❦

Our single greatest enemy may be impatience.

People recovering from chemical dependencies are highly vulnerable to the insanity of modern civilization, and therefore must be constantly vigilant.

Is modern civilization really insane? Perhaps you can explain the logic of spending extra thousands of dollars for a car that can go from 0 to 50 miles per hour in 8.3 seconds, instead of one that takes 12 seconds. Why are 4 seconds worth an additional $30,000? Why are there "instant-on" television sets to eliminate the 20 seconds of warmup? What do people do with those 20 seconds they save?

Suppose I tried to sell drugs that give a great high, but take about 48 hours to feel the effect. Would there be any customers for this drug, even if it were cheap? Would people drink alcohol if its effect didn't take place for one or two days? Addiction is the desire for instant gratification, and chemicals satisfy this need.

We have to be especially careful, because the high-tech emphasis on instantaneous results makes people less patient nowadays. For those in recovery, impatience increases the risk of relapse.

The Wisdom to Know the Difference
❧

Guilt can be healthy or unhealthy.

In the Serenity Prayer, we ask for the "wisdom to know the difference." There are many things about which we should know the difference, because if we don't, we are likely to confuse the desirable with the undesirable.

What should we do when we feel guilty? Should we seek psychiatric treatment for guilt feelings, or should we try to atone for our guilt?

Each approach has its proper place, but if we use the improper approach, everything may become confused. If the reason we feel guilty is because we actually did something wrong, whether to a family member, a friend, or against society, the proper thing to do is to make the necessary amends to set things straight. The guilt feelings from actually having done harm are healthy, requiring appropriate corrective action rather than treatment.

But sometimes we feel guilty for things we have never done, and we assume responsibility for events for which we should not feel responsible. Just as making amends for something we *did* can be very effective, making amends for something we did *not* do is not effective. The source of unwarranted guilt should be investigated, and we should seek appropriate treatment to overcome it.

Treatment and atonement each have their proper place, but it is important to know the difference.

The Gift of an Extra Day
🍎

Appropriate consideration for the future is not incompatible with "One day at a time."

Today is February 29. What would happen if we did not add an extra day every four years? Over a period of 100 years, we would fall twenty-five days behind; and over a period of 300 years, winter would extend into May or June.

So what? Why should we care today what will happen 300 years from now when we will be long gone and forgotten? If people had thought this way several hundred years ago, we would be having August weather in February.

If there is nothing we can do about the future, then trying to improve things is futile and frustrating. If we can do something, then we have the obligation to do so.

We have appropriate weather for February today because hundreds of years ago people thought about the future. We should appreciate that, and give future generations the same consideration we have been given.

By the way, you now have an extra day. Some people who receive a bonus squander it foolishly. Use your bonus day wisely.

Avoiding Setbacks
🍎

The recovery program always serves a purpose.

A wise man once said that character development is not like climbing a steep hill, but rather like pushing a wagon up a steep hill. As long as you are moving upward, you are okay, but if you stop, the wagon will roll down the hill unless you put blocks under the wheels.

There is growth in sobriety, and working the Steps in the program provides such growth. There is also a fairly constant force that threatens to pull us down. As long as we continue to grow and move up the hill, we do not have to worry too seriously about slipping.

Sometimes we reach a point where we remain stationary for a while. We seem to be treading water, and we may not feel that we are growing. At such times, the danger of slipping increases, because we temporarily do not sense upward momentum.

During such periods, the program can serve as "blocks under the wheels" to prevent us from rolling back down. It is just as important to continue intensive program involvement in these phases as when we feel we are growing. People become lax in working the recovery program when they feel they are not getting much out of it. But they are making a serious mistake. When we think we are not adding much to our development, the program serves the vital function of preventing a rollback.

Guidance is Essential

In the early phases of recovery, guidance is especially important.

A woman who was being discharged from treatment told me that she was frightened about going home. I responded that her being frightened was a positive sign, because it is when we are overconfident that we get into trouble.

"It's not that I'm afraid I'll drink again," she said. "When I started drinking at eighteen, my emotional development came to a halt. I have a daughter who is seventeen, and what is so frightening to me is that I have to function as her mother, although I am just about at her emotional age."

This is an insightful observation. Yet, it does not have to take twenty years of sobriety to make up for twenty years of arrested emotional development. With proper help, such as working the Steps of the program and competent counseling, the gap can be closed much more quickly.

Early in sobriety we operate at a level of maturity behind our chronological age. This is why it is vitally important that we take guidance and direction from people who are emotionally more mature.

All Drugs Can Be Destructive

Mood-altering chemicals are brain toxic.

A young man was brought to the psychiatric unit of our hospital in a catatonic state, mute and immobile. He was clearly schizophrenic.

The following day two people from NA came to my office and said, "Doc, we want to talk to you about Bobby. He is not psychotic."

"You don't know what you're talking about," I said. "Bobby is so catatonic that he is not able to eat or drink, and we may have to tube-feed him."

"Doc, Bobby may look crazy, but he's only crazy the way an addict is crazy. He has taken enormous amounts of chemicals for years. Don't give him the medication for schizophrenics. Keep him here where he'll be safe," they said. "He'll get better, and we will come and take him to a meeting every day."

I don't know why I let myself be talked into this, but I did not give Bob any medications, and every day two people came and carried off a rigid body to a meeting.

Bob not only improved but has been completely normal for ten years.

Psychotropic medications may be necessary to treat mental illness, but sometimes it is wise to allow the brain to regain normal function after the devastating effect of the chemicals to which it had been subjected.

The Importance of Your Sponsor
🍎

Having a sponsor is an important component of recovery.

The diseases we are involved with are alcoholism and chemicalism. The *ism* has to do with the way we think and feel, even when chemicals are not in our system. In fact, much of this thinking preceded the use of chemicals.

Part of the *ism* is that we may see things the way we would like to see them, instead of the way they are. Our minds can play tricks on us.

We need someone who can help us straighten out our distorted thinking and see things the way they really are. A sponsor is an ideal person to do this. Sponsors usually do not have the biases or personal involvement that distort our thinking, and can therefore be more objective.

Sometimes people have difficulties with their sponsors because the sponsors say things they do not want to hear. That is the best indication that you have the right person as sponsor. Hearing nice things about yourself makes you *feel* better, but it does nothing to make you get better. If you feel upset and angry because your sponsor has chastised you, call him or her and say thank you.

We Are Responsible For Our Recovery
❦

While addictions are diseases, this does not exonerate anyone from errant behavior while under the influence of chemicals.

The addictive person is not responsible for being an addict. Many people drink alcohol, but all do not become alcoholics. And some people experiment with drugs, but they do not become addicted. By analogy, many people indulge in sweets, yet they do not become diabetic. While there are obviously many differences in these conditions, the common feature is that, for the addict, something happens within the body that results in the specific symptoms of each disease. While we don't know all the causes, we do know that there are genetic and biochemical factors over which people have no control. Just as we do not think of the diabetic as responsible for her disease, neither should we hold the addict responsible for the abnormality that results in reaction to these chemicals.

However, just as diabetics must be responsible for taking their insulin or any other treatment, so addicts must be responsible for their treatment, including abstinence. As one person with many years of sobriety stated, "I may not be responsible for my disease, but I am fully responsible for my recovery."

There Are Things
We Cannot Understand
🍎

Suffering should not be interpreted as having been abandoned by God.

A few years ago a child who had undergone open-heart surgery was given a treatment consisting of suction of his trachea and bronchial tubes, a most unpleasant procedure. The child's father was not permitted in the treatment room. As the procedure began, the child struggled, kicked, and screamed, "Stop it! It's hurting me! Daddy, don't let them hurt me." Out in the corridor stood the father, wringing his hands, watching his child suffer, but knowing that he should not rush in and stop the doctors from hurting his child. He knew that the painful procedure was necessary for his child's health, and he suffered along with the child.

Like a child, we may not be able to understand how the adversities we experience could possibly be to our ultimate benefit. While we cannot change many things, and must turn to a Higher Power, we should have the security that comes with knowing that the Higher Power does not abandon us. When we suffer, He suffers with us.

Learning From Adversity
❦

John consulted me because he was having a very difficult day. He had been sober for thirty-two years, and had no one to turn to because he had outlived all his sponsors. He admitted that he felt himself very close to relapse.

John was surprised to hear that what was happening to him was beneficial. I pointed out that, although I had often called him for recommendations of people who could help a newcomer, I had never asked him to do so.

I told John that many people who need help are struggling with temptation and are experiencing intense discomfort. They may be helped by someone who can identify with their feelings. However, since John's struggle against the temptation to drink had long since passed, his usefulness to a newcomer was limited.

John dealt with his crisis by increasing the frequency of meetings, and doing the kinds of things that a newcomer is advised to do. He later confided that his sobriety had taken on a new quality after this episode.

When difficult days occur to people who have had years of abstinence, there is no reason to panic. These may be episodes of rejuvenation, which stimulate growth in sobriety and increase one's effectiveness in helping others.

Anger
🍎

A gentleman who was admitted for rehabilitation from alcoholism was so angry that other residents were afraid of him.

On interview, it was evident that this man was struggling to avoid crying. In the privacy of my office, I said to him, "It's okay to cry when you're hurt. I promise I won't tell anyone that you cried." He promptly broke down in uncontrollable sobbing.

This man's anger was not hostility directed toward someone but, rather, was a desperate attempt to conceal his true feelings. He had been hurt deeply, but for whatever reason he could not acknowledge his pain, let alone express it. After all, big men do not hurt, let alone cry.

This man's psychological system converted his pain to anger. Since it is absurd to feel angry with someone without reason, he would find trivial things to justify his anger. These were weak rationalizations to account for a feeling he could not express in any other way.

Whether we feel angry toward others or we think others feel angry toward us, we should ask ourselves: Is this anger legitimate, or is it a result of some other feeling that is being denied? If someone seems hostile, we should consider the possibility that the anger is not directed toward us, and avoid reacting defensively. If we feel angry toward another, we should realize that this anger may be unjust, and learn to acknowledge our true feelings.

Recognizing God's Presence
❦

Hallucinations can be either negative or positive.

Seeing something that is *not* real is a positive hallucination. Not seeing something that *is* real is a negative hallucination.

If we hear God's voice, that is a positive hallucination. If we do not perceive God's communication, that is a negative hallucination.

God communicates with us in many ways. He does so through the vastness of the universe, the intricacies of a leaf as seen under the microscope, the bright colors of tropical fish, the unparalleled dazzling colors of the leaves in autumn, and the trill of the nightingale. He communicates with us through the people who are placed in our way, and from whom we can learn if we only try. He communicates with us through the sublime thoughts and emotions generated by our souls.

Perhaps the difference between the Prophets of yore and ourselves is that when they received the Divine word they said, "I am here and I am ready"—Genesis 22:1. We, too, may hear ourselves being called to a mission, but we may not respond to the roll call.

Turning our life over to a Higher Power is our way of saying, "I am here, I am ready." Once we sincerely make that statement, we can receive the Divine communication.

The Blame Game

We need to take corrective action, and not to blame.

There are four essentials for human life: food and water, clothing, shelter, and someone to blame.

While blaming others is widespread, one can only wonder, what purpose does it serve? Hunger tells us the body needs nourishment, and the sensation of cold tells us we need clothes or shelter, but what function can blaming someone serve?

Blaming can relieve us of the burden of doing something about our situation. If we can point out whose fault something is, it releases us from the need to change. The reasoning goes, "Let the person whose fault it is correct the situation. Why should I? I didn't cause it."

Strangely, if someone set fire to your home, you would do whatever necessary to put out the fire, even though you knew who started it. Why not act similarly when our behavior requires change? It is typical for an addict to blame others: "If only they would stop doing these irritating things to me, I would not need to drink or use." Rather than make the necessary changes in behavior, the addict blames others, which appears to absolve him or her from change.

It is wise to eliminate blame in recovery. We need not blame ourselves or others. Our emphasis should be on what is necessary to recover.

Real Change Takes Time
❦

Addiction and recovery are both progressive phenomena.

Especially when the chemical is alcohol, addiction often begins with what appears to be safe, social drinking, and progresses insidiously. Denial prevents a person from realizing what is happening, and the progression may last for decades. The moment of truth may come suddenly. In a moment of insight, a person realizes what has been going on for many years.

When the addict recovers, the reflection may not relate back to the many years the disease progressed, but to the suddenness of the realization. Rather than understand that recovery is a long and progressive process, just as was the development of the disease, the expectation is that it will be quick—just like the moment of insight.

The addict may expect instantaneous recovery. With the chemical eliminated, everything should change rapidly. He may expect everyone's attitude to change as radically as his own.

We must realize that, even with the chemical gone, character traits take time to change. The recovering addict should not lose patience with himself, and should certainly not have unrealistic expectations of others.

The Twelve Steps of recovery are steps, not a high-speed escalator. The slogan, "time takes time" means that there is no microwave for recovery.

Make a Contribution

Addiction and recovery are both unique phenomena.

While there are many similarities among chemically dependent people, there are also many differences. Each individual's history of addiction and recovery is as unique as one's fingerprints.

This uniqueness is why it is so important that recovering people frequently attend AA or NA meetings. Over and above what one gets, there is much that one can give.

There may be someone trying to recover who needs to hear what *you* have to say. It is your particular story—one particular incident, or one observation that you made. It will elicit a response in one individual. And even if the event was not unique, it may be the way you describe it that triggers another person's recovery.

One woman related that she had difficulty identifying with the program until she heard a speaker say, "This is the first time out of my house for two months, following my operation for cancer. This program helped me to get through the ordeal, because it helped me live my life as it is rather than as I would like it to be." This particular idea and the way it was phrased touched this woman's needs.

We all have something unique to contribute. We should not withhold it from others.

Learn to Trust
❧

Developing trust is crucial in sobriety.

Some chemically dependent people grew up in the home of an addicted parent, and may have COA (Children of Addicts) issues to deal with.

Growing up in the home of an addicted parent can leave emotional scars. There may have been no manifestation of love from a parent who was too sick to show love or who was preoccupied with controlling the spouse's addiction. There may have been no rudiments of trust in a home where nothing was predictable. If you had to assume adult responsibilities early in life, you may have missed a normal childhood. You may have felt shame—an intolerable feeling that somehow you are just not good enough, regardless of what you do.

Because these feelings are part of our development, they may seem so natural that we don't recognize how destructive they can be. We are unable to rid ourselves of resentment if we do not even know what the resentment is. People try to turn their lives over to God, or they try to confide in another, but seem unable to do so. They do not realize that they are unable to trust either God or another person—because they never learned how to trust.

Attending meetings of Children of Addicts can improve your own recovery by helping remove some of the obstacles to effective working of the Twelve Steps.

True Relationships Don't Come Easily
❦

Chemically dependent people often have problems with relationships.

One person reacted to this statement with, "I never had any trouble with relationships. I've had one relationship, only it has been with thirty different people." How can a person have one kind of relationship with thirty different people? Relationships should all be unique.

A relationship between two people is a give and take. Each person reacts to the other, and there is flexibility, whereby each gives and receives, and both become enriched. When a relationship is in only one direction, it is not a relationship at all. For instance, we can hardly call eating a "relationship" between ourselves and our food. We simply eat the food, and that's all there is to it. We give nothing of ourselves to the food.

Some people relate to others only by taking. Whether they seek sex, money, security, or dependency, it is always the same. Others can relate only by giving, and are reluctant to accept anything—perhaps because they feel undeserving or because accepting something obligates them. If we are only taking or only giving, what occurs is the same thing repeatedly. We become so rigid that we lose all capacity for adjustment, and we repeat the same situation thirty times, which is hardly a relationship. Life becomes monotonous and boring.

Learn to give of yourself, to accept from others, and to be flexible. You can have a truly meaningful relationship.

Learning From Hard Times
🍎

The seeds of happiness sometimes root in episodes of distress.

Not many people get through life without adversity. When we are in distress, we hurt so badly that we have only one thought: "I want relief now!" When we experience suffering, we can hardly philosophize about the ultimate good it may bring.

After our painful ordeal is over, and we can look back upon what happened, we have the option of being resentful and angry toward God or of looking objectively at what happened. We may discover that the very things we felt to be so terrible were the seeds of subsequent growth and progress.

A person who has never heard of farming once visited a farm, and when he saw the farmer sowing grain, he remarked, "How stupid! He is taking perfectly good kernels of grain and burying them in the ground." The abundant crop that would come out of this would not be apparent until months later. Having no knowledge of what would come from the planting, he thought it to be foolish.

Even at times of distress, we should bear in mind that the very darkness of suffering is where we are most apt to find our Higher Power.

Unconditional Love

True love should be unconditional.

A member of a therapy group once remarked, "My parents' definition of love was 'love is doing what you're told to do.' " Others laughed, but some nodded knowingly because they, too, had grown up with the understanding that love is doing what you are told.

But how can people be so mixed up? Doing what one is told to do is *obedience*, not love. People who are in someone's employ must do what they are told, but what does this have to do with love?

If people we love do something self-destructive, we try to stop them. When they hurt, we hurt. If we try to stop them from harming themselves, it is not because we wish to control them but because we love them. If they pay no attention and go on harming themselves, we feel their pain. We may be angry, but we do not love them any less. We cannot condone or reward self-destructive behavior because that would contribute to their destruction. But unconditional love means loving even when we are disappointed or angry.

Will others know we love them when we act in their best interests? Even if they do not recognize our love right then, some day they will.

Changing Our Whole Life
❧

In Step Twelve we say "to practice these principles in all our affairs."

There are some things we do by reflex and others out of habit. If something comes flying toward our face, we blink. When we walk, we put one foot in front of the other out of habit. We could control blinking and we could think about each step, but we would go crazy if we brought these actions under voluntary control.

When it comes to the mouth and tongue, we could exercise much *more* voluntary control. If we let our mouths work by reflex or habit, we can harm ourselves and others. Speech is one behavior we should subject to conscious deliberation.

During active addiction, we often drink or use chemicals out of habit. We deceive ourselves in thinking these are voluntary acts. The disease has taken them out of our control. It is only when we realize that we have totally lost control, and turn our lives over to a Higher Power, that we can replace a defective control system with one that works.

Chemical use may not be the only part of our life that is out of control. Sobriety goes beyond abstinence. It requires that we look at the totality of our lives. If we find some behaviors are out of control—speech, for example—we can first try to bring that under control. But if that is not possible, we should look for a Higher Power to help us.

It's Not All Your Fault

There is some confusion about guilt.

A recovering person stated that he was having a difficult time with guilt. His wife was mentally ill with a paranoid psychosis, and he felt that his drinking had caused this. He had prayed for God to relieve him of this guilt, but this had not helped.

I told the man that he was in error. "You cannot cause another person to become psychotic. Your wife's mental illness was not the cause of your alcoholism, nor was your drinking the cause of her mental illness." No person is so powerful that he or she can make another person either psychotic or alcoholic.

When we regret having done something wrong, but still feel guilty after making amends, we can ask God's forgiveness to remove the painful feelings of guilt. This is appropriate and it works. However, while we should feel guilt for having harmed another, if it is clear that we are *not* responsible for another person's disease, there are no grounds for guilt. Asking God to relieve *that* guilt is just as though we were holding on to a live electric wire and asking God to remove the electric shock. God's answer would be, "Let go of the wire."

It is foolish to hold onto a live wire and pray not to be shocked. Similarly, if we hold on to guilt that we have no business having, and ask God to lift that burden of guilt, He may say, "Just put it down. You had no business picking it up."

Faith and Effort Make a Difference
❧

Faith and action are the ideal combination.

The psalmist says, "Trust in God and do good"—
Psalms 37:3. Total reliance on God, to the extent that
we make no effort on our own behalf, will not succeed.
This is not the teaching of religion. It is much like the
pastor who complimented the farmer on the acres of
land that were handsomely adorned with rows of vegetables. "I see that you and the Lord are doing a wonderful
job," he said. The farmer acquiesced, but said, "I wish
you'd seen it when the Lord was running it by Himself."

While our own efforts are essential, they are not always sufficient. Without Divine rain, our plowing, till-
ing, and seeding would produce nothing. The Divine
blessing of the work of our hands brings us the results
we seek.

Sometimes we refrain from undertaking a project because it appears too formidable. If it is the right thing to
do, we should not be frightened away by a challenge,
and we should trust that God will help bring our efforts
to successful completion.

Sobriety is a challenge that requires our maximum
effort. But having seen so many times that our own
efforts fall short, we invoke Divine assistance. This approach should not be restricted to recovery from addiction. It can be applied with equal success to many other
challenges in life.

Meetings Are Life-Savers
❦

One woman called four months after completing treatment to report that she was still sober, but that she had stopped going to AA because she did not enjoy the meetings. I asked this woman what she would think of a person who had cancer that required radiation treatments, but who refused them because she didn't enjoy them.

Isn't it ludicrous to reject a life-saving treatment because you do not enjoy it? I had not prescribed AA meetings as a social hour or amusement. If she was looking for enjoyment, she could try an entertaining movie. The woman had to realize that she had an addictive disease—potentially fatal if untreated. The proper treatment includes AA meetings, and these meetings are effective whether one enjoys them or not.

Several months later the woman called to report that she had gone back to AA and was sober. She realized that she had the wrong expectations of AA. She added that once she saw the meetings as a treatment for her disease, she actually began enjoying them.

There is nothing wrong with taking a potent antibiotic that has a pleasant flavor. But we must recognize that we are not taking the medicine for its flavor, but for its life-saving action. Similarly, there is nothing wrong with enjoying an AA or NA meeting, but we must be aware that these meetings are necessary to arrest the otherwise inexorable process of addiction.

Know Yourself

Why is self-awareness important in recovery?

A healthy and successful adjustment to life is contingent upon a correct perception of reality. For example, a person who is very wealthy and spends a great deal of money is not likely to get into any trouble, whereas a person of meager means who has a delusion that he is a multimillionaire is going to get into a great deal of trouble. Similarly, a person of limited intellect who realizes his limitations is quite apt to adjust to his reality. But a gifted person who perceives herself as less adequate than she really is is apt to have many problems. Addiction is commonly characterized by such negative self-perceptions.

Shakespeare was so right when he said, "This above all, to thine own self be true." If we do not have a correct concept of our own selves, then we are misperceiving the most important element of reality: ourselves.

The Twelve Step program helps bring about a more accurate self-perception. The Fourth and Fifth Steps lay the groundwork, and the Tenth Step carries it forward. Of course, all the other Steps contribute significantly to building self-esteem so that the new personality emerges —the real personality, the one whose existence we were unaware of even before chemical use began.

Learn to Adapt

Adaptability is essential for happiness.

We pray for "the courage to change the things we can." Change means adaptation, and good sobriety requires the capacity to adapt. Chemical use is often aggravated by rigidity, as when we have the attitude, "I am the way I am, and the world should change to suit me."

If we do not learn how to adapt, we are certain to become frustrated. For example, some parents may become upset when their children mature, because they now feel useless, no longer needed.

Parents are *always* needed, although the character of the need changes. When children are infants, parents must diaper and feed them. As they grow, parents must provide for their children and guide them through their development. Even when children become financially independent and are detached from their parents, the parents still serve a valuable purpose. Parents' roles change, but never cease.

Just as we must be flexible and adapt to this kind of change, we must adapt to other changes in life. If we remain fixed, we are certain to be disillusioned. As we grow in sobriety, we can minimize the disappointments in life as we improve our ability to adapt.

Sobriety Is a Gift of God
❦

Sobriety is a Divine gift.

Recovering people may tell their therapists, "Thank you for saving my life." This is pleasant to hear, but we should recognize the truth. We can be so easily deceived, especially when we wish to be.

Two practical jokers once visited Yellowstone National Park, where Old Faithful geyser has been erupting every 65 minutes since time immemorial. They obtained a steering wheel from a junkyard, and placed themselves near Old Faithful, where they could be seen by visitors. They stuck the shaft of the steering wheel into the ground, and waited until the guide explained to tourists how Old Faithful never failed to erupt, to the second.

About five seconds before the eruption, one joker shouted loudly to his friend, "Okay Frank, let her go!" and the other man gave the steering wheel a few vigorous turns, just as the geyser shot up. Onlookers might have thought the eruption was brought about by opening a valve. The truth was that it had nothing to do with it.

We do many things to guide people to sobriety, and when they succeed, they often give us full credit for the achievement. The truth is that sobriety is not achieved by our own efforts, whether client or therapist. Sobriety is a gift of God. Recovering people can make themselves able to accept that gift, and helpers can show how to stop obstructing God's gift.

Let Go of the Past
❦

What can we do about the past?

Newcomers to AA or NA may remark, "I must be in the wrong place. If everyone is sober, how come they are smiling? I haven't had a chemical for eight days and I am absolutely miserable." Their bewilderment increases when they hear a speaker relate a rather unpleasant experience of the past, and then join with the audience in laughter as though it were a rib-tickling comedy.

The attitude of AA and NA reflects the Serenity Prayer, and is the converse of the way most of the world operates. The program requires that we be earnest about the present and immediate future. The things we can do something about must be approached with a profound sense of responsibility. Taking one day at a time, we can concentrate all our thoughts and energies on that day. Few things about today are trivial.

The attitude changes drastically in regard to the past. We cannot make yesterday any better. If we obsess on the mistakes of the past, it results in depression or the kind of "pity party" that is conducive to relapse. Inasmuch as whether we laugh or cry, the past will not change, so people in the program choose to laugh.

Do recovering people take life seriously? Of course. They take it so seriously that they cannot dissipate limited energies on futile exercises, such as bewailing the past.

Avoid Codependence

"Detaching" from an addict is not abandonment.

A doctor may instruct a heart patient to exercise and engage in sports, but not in competitive sports. This is because in competitive sports such as tennis, we do not set our own pace; we respond to the pace set by the other player. When we exercise on our own, we can slow down if we feel weary or in pain. When we respond to the pace set by another person, we cannot stop when our warning signals tell us that we are going too far.

This is equally true of codependents. Codependents do not steer a course for themselves. Rather, they react to the addict's behavior.

Codependents can be dragged along only if tightly attached. If the disease that runs the addict's life also runs you as a codependent, your life can become chaotic. Detachment does not mean you are deserting the addict or severing all relations. It simply means you are avoiding being dragged along. Family members may be frightened by the term *detachment*. "How can I detach from him, especially if he has a disease? How can I walk away from a sick person who may need my help?" A correct understanding of detachment eliminates this concern. We recognize that the other person has a disease, and we relate to him as long as *we* set the pace of the relationship.

Fear of Intimacy
🌿

Chemically dependent people often have a problem with intimacy.

True intimacy is contingent upon self-esteem. If we think there is something terribly wrong with us, we are likely to avoid relating to other people, for fear that they may discover our defects and reject or ridicule us. To avoid this pain, we avoid people.

Sometimes this avoidance is total and we avoid all relationships, becoming loners. Sometimes we feel that social relationships are safe, because we can act in a manner such that other people will not discover our fantasied defects. But when it comes to intimacy, this is not possible. We cannot successfully put on an act for a long-term, intimate relationship.

How many couples do you know who enjoyed a wonderful relationship until one of them began to talk about getting serious? How many couples had a fabulous courtship, only to have a fallout soon after marriage? Such happenings are invariably the result of a fear that intimacy will expose the true self. If we are ashamed of our true selves, such exposure can indeed be frightening.

We need to realize that the self of which we are so ashamed is but a figment of our imagination. If only we could get to know our true selves, we would have a much different opinion of ourselves and would no longer be reluctant to let others discover who we truly are.

Live One Day at a Time
❦

What does it mean to live one day at a time?

"One day at a time" does not mean doing today only that which is useful today. If we spend time in training to enable us to eventually earn a living, or if we put away money in a pension fund for our retirement, that is not a violation of one day at a time. If we try to correct a mistake of the past by making amends, that is not a violation of one day at a time. Doing something today to prepare for the future or to compensate for the past is perfectly okay.

However, if we worry about either a past or future event that we can do nothing about, that is a violation of one day at a time—for example, after taking a final exam, if we worry about what the grade might be. All the worry in the world will not change that grade. Or if we worry about another person's behavior over which we have no control. Or if we think today about how we are going to deal with the urge to drink next holiday season. "One day at a time" simply means dealing today with something we can do something about, and leaving alone those things we can do nothing about.

Perhaps people who do not ascribe to "one day at a time" have a secret method for doing something about things they can do nothing about. Could they please come forward and share this with the rest of us?

Like Yourself
🍎

Liking oneself is essential for sobriety.

I once vacationed at a spa for respite from unrelenting stress at work. My first contact with a whirlpool bath was one of sheer bliss.

After several minutes I emerged from the tub, remarking how wonderful it had been. I was instructed to return for twenty minutes more, because that was the prescribed regimen. After about five minutes I made it known that I had had it; only the threat that lack of compliance would disqualify me for the full treatment returned me to the bath for fifteen minutes that were virtually intolerable.

Why was I unable to tolerate relaxation? Perhaps because while we are all expert at enjoying diversions, such as music, television, books, or sports, few of us can truly relax, which means lying back with our eyes closed yet not asleep, just enjoying being by ourselves.

Being alone in the bath, with nothing to read, or listen to, or look at, and no one to talk to, left me in the sole company of myself. If you are alone in the company of someone you do not like, you become uneasy. Without anything to divert me from myself, I simply did not like the company I was in, because I did not like myself!

If we like ourselves, we can relax without brain depressing chemicals. Recovery helps us like ourselves.

Honesty

Sobriety requires rigorous honesty.

Addiction is full of deceit: lying, cheating, coverups. In recovery, it is essential to abandon dishonesty and become truthful, even if it hurts. Abstinence without honesty is not sobriety—and is virtually certain to lead to relapse.

Truthfulness can become an excellent guide to living. For example, when we are in doubt about whether or not to do something, just reflect: "If I do this particular thing, will I ever be in a position where I may have to deny it?" If so, don't do it!

We should always be proud of what we have done. True pride is constructive. Only false pride is destructive. False pride prevents us from admitting our powerlessness and from taking a moral inventory. It prevents us from making amends and from humbly asking God to remove our character defects. With false pride we cannot be humble or admit that we have any character defects.

But with true pride we realize that we are too precious to allow anything to detract from our beauty. People who own something valuable take great care of it. True pride prevents self-ruination by chemicals, and will not allow us to do anything beneath our dignity.

Honesty and true pride can make life much easier. At the end of each day we can feel good about what we have done and not make excuses.

Learn to Feel Again

In recovery we must deal with feelings.

Many people admit difficulty in managing negative feelings: anger, hatred, grief, or envy. But they may not perceive why they need help with feelings such as pride, joy, or being loved. I frequently encounter people who have difficulty in accepting love or feeling happy. It seems as though feelings of *any* kind pose a problem for them.

Think of it this way. A faucet in your bathroom breaks, and water gushes all over the place. You can't find the valve to shut off the water. In desperation you shut off the valve that controls the water supply to the entire house. This is what can happen with feelings. People who are unable to deal with anger do not know how to turn off their angry feelings, and may, therefore, they shut off *all* their feelings.

When we help the recovering person manage feelings, we open the feeling system again. This flood of feelings may cause much confusion and anxiety, and can be one of the reasons for relapse into chemicals.

In recovery we must realize that discontinuing use of chemicals will release all kinds of feelings, and that even love and joy may give us problems. We must have patience in learning how to deal with our feelings.

Resentment

We grow through stress.

Think of the most enjoyable experience you have ever had, and what you have learned from it. Now think about what you have learned from some painful experiences. We rarely learn from pleasant experiences; it is the painful ones that teach us something.

Painful experiences not only teach us what to avoid but also make us turn to others for help. They bring us closer to others. They make us pray, and bring us closer to God. They sensitize us to others who suffer, so we can empathize and extend help wherever possible. Thus, our character develops more as a result of painful experiences than of enjoyable ones.

Cows in the pasture appear to be content. People, too, may seek contentment—but is that really our ultimate goal? If someone guaranteed us a life of contentment, we would seize the opportunity. But should contentment really be our goal? What growth would there be if we were always content? The human soul can survive only if it grows, and growth comes at the price of suffering.

While you are working on resentments, just remember this. The things we resent the most may be those that give us our greatest growth.

Trust Brings Change
🍎

Sobriety constitutes a new way of life.

For newly recovering addicts, sobriety means abandoning the only way of life they have known and adopting a new, totally unfamiliar way. This may be frightening, and the only thing that can diminish this fear is trust in someone who offers guidance.

Trust is an important concept, vital to recovery. But for many people trust is an unknown. They have found that each time they trusted, they were hurt. Too often trust has led to disappointment. People who feel unable to trust anyone have decided to do everything themselves.

Many addicts are children of addicts. Being the child of an addicted parent can leave you without a sense of trust. Addicted parents are likely to make many promises they do not keep. These parents can be unpredictable, so that the child learns never to rely on anything.

The basis of trust is a loving child-parent relationship. When that foundation is lacking, subsequent development of trust is inadequate. But you can begin to learn trust with a caring, competent therapist. In AA and NA you will find people who can be trusted. As trust increases, you find people who can guide you to a new way of living.

Make a Daily Effort
🍎

Sobriety requires constant vigilance.

We often hear the term "90 in 90"—the advice given to newcomers to attend an AA or NA meeting daily for ninety days. A person might infer, however, that after three months he or she no longer needs AA or NA every day.

While it is possible, with a solid foundation in recovery, to decrease from daily meetings, it is not possible to stay sober unless we practice at least *some* aspect of the program each day. Each morning we pray for another day of sobriety, and every night we give thanks for having had another day of sobriety. In addition every day we inventory ourselves, make amends, help other people, and stay in touch with our sponsor.

Chemicals are enemies—cunning, baffling, and powerful enemies. A cunning enemy is not going to destroy us today with tactics used on us previously, because we know how to defend ourselves against them. A cunning enemy seeks new ways to defeat us, constantly searching for vulnerabilities. The help we received from the program yesterday was effective in dealing with yesterday's enemy, but the tactics will not work today because the enemy has a new strategy.

Daily meetings are an effective way to counter the enemy's tactics. If we are unable to attend daily meetings, we do something else to reinforce the program. The cunning, baffling, and powerful enemy never lets up.

Keep Coming Back. It Works
❧

A familiar AA and NA aphorism is, "Keep coming back. It works!"

Psychologists may theorize on the dynamics of addiction, and some apply these theories to treatment, but the results of these approaches are not gratifying. They may indeed be logical, but addiction is not a logical condition.

I once had the pleasure of attending a friend's twentieth anniversary of sobriety. He reminisced about his early days in the program when, in spite of regular attendance, he was unable to stay sober more than a few weeks. He asked one of the veterans in AA, "Just what is it that I'm doing wrong?"

The old-timer answered, "Son, you're trying to analyze this program too much. If you want to get better, just follow instructions and stop asking why."

"That was anathema to me," my friend said. "After all, I am an attorney, an intelligent person. I've never done anything in my life without understanding why I am doing it.

"Then I reflected," he continued, "there must be something that these guys are doing right that I am not doing. They are staying sober and I am getting drunk. Against my better judgment, I decided to experiment and just try it their way. As a result of this experiment, I am now twenty years sober."

Leave the theorizing to those who can afford it. The only reason why an addict should work the program, and the only sensible reason, is: it works.

Don't Get Hooked on Failure

In my book *When Do the Good Things Start?* I have a "Peanuts" cartoon showing Charlie Brown saying to Lucy, "I've just been reading about the decline and fall of the Roman Empire. I also read about the decline of Hollywood, the decline of popular music, the decline of family life, the decline of imperialism, the decline of morality, the decline of boxing. I've always been fascinated by failure."

Some people have adjusted to a life of failure, and are more comfortable with failure than with success. This is prevalent in chemically dependent people, for example. They embark on a new venture and, just about when it is to reach fruition, they do something to sabotage it.

This adjustment to failure comes from the fear that success will bring additional responsibilities. A successful venture may indeed create new responsibilities. On the other hand, once it fails, we don't have to worry about responsibilities. Or we may think that we do not deserve success and feel guilty when something goes right. We see failure as our just dessert.

In either case, this attitude can be traced to negative feelings about ourselves. Responsibilities are feared because we do not feel adequate to meet the challenge. Good things are feared because feelings of worthlessness make us feel guilty.

Working a good recovery program can correct a negative self-image and help us achieve success.

Recovery and Fellowship

Recovery entitles you to membership in the world's finest fellowship.

The equality that prevails in meeting rooms is refreshing. Once in the room, a person's economic status makes no difference. When the basket is passed, no one cares whether you put in fifty cents or fifty dollars. For that matter, it is jokingly said that if someone is in dire straits, and must take out fifty cents, everyone will understand.

In organized religions, churches and temples have budgets that must be met, and are invariably financed by contributions from the membership. A church or temple can hardly afford to offend or alienate an influential member who makes a major contribution, and the member may be shown some favoritism. But in an anonymous fellowship, there is no way anyone can gain greater influence, and thus there is true equality.

It is tragic that so many wars have been fought over religious differences, with each side insisting that their religion is *the* true one, and that their God is greatest. But I have never heard anyone say, "My Higher Power is greater than your Higher Power."

Seeing the anonymous fellowship as only for abstinence from chemicals does not give it its full due. If we consider the unique spirit of equality that exists in the fellowship, doesn't the rest of the world have much to learn from it?

Teach Your Children Well
❧

Addiction-prevention programs have not been a smashing success.

Providing information about chemicals is not enough, and scare techniques do not work. The week basketball star Len Bias died of cocaine, premium cocaine was peddled as "Len Bias quality."

We might approach prevention by considering the causes of addiction: the genetic, physiological, social, psychological, and spiritual factors.

We cannot change our genes, and the physiological causes of addiction are not yet sufficiently elucidated to yield to manipulation. Social changes are difficult to make. Although we can avoid "people, places, and things," we must be careful not to confuse this with a geographic cure.

What we can modify are psychological factors: building self-esteem and developing effective coping skills. And we can change the spiritual factors: better values in life and mastery over our biological drives.

The psychological and spiritual ingredients must come from the home. Children adopt their parents' values; parents are the first instructors in coping skills. Children who see their parents escaping from problems instead of coping will copy this pattern, regardless of whether the parents were escaping by chemicals, food, or any other method that avoids coping with reality.

Preventive measures must begin at home.

No Man Is an Island

There is a commonality in addiction.

Some addicts have particularly intense feelings of uniqueness. This is especially true of professional people, who may think that because they are doctors, lawyers, or ministers they should be able to control all aspects of their lives. "I don't know of any other professional person who has this problem. What would my patients (clients, parishioners) think if they knew I am an addict?"

Addictions are diseases, not a failure of willpower or an indication of a weak personality. Would anyone be surprised that a surgeon has a hernia or that an ophthalmologist wears glasses?

Even if the public does not see these conditions as diseases, the afflicted person and his family must understand this. "Terminal uniqueness," or hanging on to the notion that "I am different and no one can understand me," is an obstacle to recovery.

Of course, we are different—but so what? We feel and think differently. Our facial features are different. There are no two human beings with identical fingerprints. Yet we use the same antibiotics for infections and undergo the same surgery for appendicitis.

Do not become a victim of terminal uniqueness. What has worked so well for others will work for you, too.

A Eulogy

The following is from a eulogy written by a person recovering from cocaine.

"I suppose that in parting I should say how much I love you, but all I can say is, 'I hate you.' You deceived me. You promised to make the world pleasant for me and I believed you. You did not tell me that your help would be brief, and that afterward I would feel worse than ever. You played games with me and teased me. You never did make me as comfortable as you did at first.

"My wife and children resented my love affair with you. They said they would leave me unless I gave you up. You told me not to worry, that you would give me more than my family ever could. Again you deceived me.

"You took everything away from me: the love of my family, my home, my job, my friends, my dignity.

"I would have still pursued you, but I had no energy left. I was crushed, broken in body, mind, and spirit. Yet, even at this moment when I bury you, you threaten to come out from the grave and haunt me. You are a liar. You never wanted to make me happy.

"I shall struggle along, trying to regain my strength, whatever is left that you did not take. I hate you, cocaine. I once loved you more than anything in the world, but now I hate you."

Answered Prayers

Sometimes we wonder if our prayers are being heard.

We regularly pray, "God grant me the serenity to accept that which I cannot change, the courage to change that which I can, and the wisdom to know the difference."

A merchant asked his wealthy friend for a loan. The friend agreed to the request. "I'll be home tonight," he said. "You may come for the money then."

That night the merchant failed to show, and the following day he approached his friend again. "I told you I would give it to you," the man said. "I waited for you last night, but you never came. I will be home again tonight, and you may come for the money."

After the merchant failed to appear for a second and third time, his friend became angry. "What kind of game are you playing with me?" he asked. If you want the money, then come for it, and if you don't, then quit pestering me for it."

We pray to God: Give us serenity, courage, and wisdom. Perhaps God *is* giving it to us, but we fail to take it. After all, He is only going to *grant* these to us. He does not force us to use them.

As we pray the Serenity Prayer, let us also think, think, think. Do we use the serenity, courage, and wisdom that God makes available to us?

Powerlessness

Powerlessness is not unique to addiction.

I once had a terrifying experience. The shortest route to the hospital was down a steep hill. When the hill was icy, the police would set up barricades. One day, seeing no barricades, I reasoned that the hill must be safe. It was not and, try as I might, I could not stop the car or steer it into the curb. At the foot of the hill was a busy thoroughfare, and I knew I was about to be killed. It was only by the grace of God that I slipped through that busy intersection unharmed.

One young man asked me, "Why didn't you just jump out of the car?"

As I thought about his question, the answer became obvious. I did not jump out of the car because I kept on trying to control it. Even though my life was in danger, I stayed in the car trying to control the uncontrollable.

Addicts are not the only people who cling to the illusion of control. But when addicts recover, they have an advantage because they now recognize their powerlessness. Though other people may have the same problem, they have not been in a recovery program, and do not realize that they are trying to control the uncontrollable.

This is what is meant by practicing the principles of the Twelve Steps in *all* our affairs.

How Codependency Develops

How do codependent relationships develop?

Suppose that, as a child, I received positive strokes only when I did something for someone else. I learned that, in order to get approval and feel good about myself, I must do things for others.

Much later, when I met you, I discovered that you have phobias—namely, you are afraid to drive or go anywhere by yourself. You have needs, and I can provide these needs. I can drive you and accompany you wherever you have to go. This satisfies my need to feel needed, and our relationship grows stronger.

I then am promoted at work to a position of authority and leadership. I begin to get enough positive strokes at work so that I no longer have so great a need to feel needed at home. Your constant demands on me begin to be a drain. "Why don't you get help with your phobias? Why don't you learn how to drive? You can't expect me to go everywhere with you. I have important business meetings to attend." I fail to realize that for many years I have been encouraging your dependence on me. When I develop other sources of input, you are left stranded.

This is an example of how a relationship deteriorates when one member undergoes a change and there is no commensurate change in the other.

Your self-esteem should not be totally dependent on another's opinion.

There Are No Substitutes
for the Program

🍋

Counseling and therapy are valuable, but they are not a substitute for the Twelve Step program.

Much has happened in the field of addiction. We have learned so much about the addictive personality, and the emotional repairs that need to be made, that we may lose sight of the two basics: don't pick up the chemical and do go to meetings.

People who resist going to the anonymous fellowship for whatever reason may circumvent the program via individual therapy. Even if the therapy is with a competent addiction counselor, it is not likely to succeed.

A man had been told that his dress was incomplete without a necktie. A fire broke out while he was bathing one day, and he grabbed a necktie and ran out of the house. When he was criticized for running out without any covering, he protested, "But I wore a necktie just as you told me." "Oh, you fool!" people said to him. "If you are wearing a shirt and pants, then the necktie is important in completing your garb, but to wear only a necktie and nothing else is ridiculous."

So it is with counseling and therapy. These are indeed valuable adjuncts to a recovery program, but therapy without the program is like a necktie on a nude body.

The Wisdom to Know the Difference

❦

The Serenity Prayer should not be modified.

Some people *say*, "God, grant me the serenity to accept that which I cannot change, the courage to change that which I can, and the wisdom to know the difference." But they *think*, "Please make some more things changeable."

In my book *When Do the Good Things Start?* Lucy tells Charlie Brown, "I never want to see you again, Charlie Brown. Never, never, never!" Charlie Brown then says, "Please define 'never.'"

There are some things we must learn to accept as finalities. For example, a woman may terminate a relationship, but her partner refuses to accept this. He may do some highly counterproductive things in a desperate attempt to resurrect the relationship. There have been instances where the recalcitrant partner has broken into the home and tried to force himself on the other person.

Some things are unchangeable. Even if some things are changeable, *we* may not be able to bring about the change. We ask for the serenity to accept "that which *I* cannot change."

The spouse may wish the addict to change, but while recovery is certainly possible, that change must be initiated by the addict. We cannot change anyone else. We are happier if we can direct our limited energies to those things that *can* be changed.

The Big Picture
❦

Being overly sensitive can cause unnecessary distress.

A woman was upset by her performance evaluation at work. She had achieved high scores in every area except one, which was noted as requiring improvement. She saw this favorable evaluation as negative because of that single deficiency.

This reminds me of a similar experience. I had delivered a lecture at a conference, after which the attendees were required to evaluate the speakers. Of the 110 people who attended, all the evaluations were complimentary except one. This was shattering to me. Never mind that 109 people had given me raving reviews; I was obsessed with the one negative comment.

I should have concluded that 109 to 1 is overwhelming—that this one dissenting person simply had poor judgment and was unable to appreciate what everyone else did. But like the woman's reaction to her evaluation, my sensitivities were such that I was offended. If you have a painful infection on one finger, you are oblivious to the fact that you have nine other healthy fingers.

We should focus on how okay we really are. In the event of a negative comment, give it due attention. If it has validity, we can improve ourselves and become even better. If it has no validity, we should not let it affect us.

Abstinence Is an Affirmative Act

❦

There is a positive approach to abstinence.

There is natural resistance to restrictions of any kind, even if self-imposed. The statement "Don't drink" or "Don't pick up" often triggers an automatic reaction to do so.

However, instead of seeing restrictions in a negative light, we can make a *positive* commitment to care for our body. We can vow not to allow harmful things to happen to it, much the same as a mother is committed to protecting her infant. Our statement is not "I am against chemicals." It is "I am *for* my body."

Like an infant, our body is entrusted into our care and is quite helpless. We can put nutritious substances into it and keep it strong; or give it dangerous chemicals, which will ruin it. Our body has no choice, and is completely at our mercy.

While our body is a vital part of our person, it is only *part* of it. We are the people in charge of our bodies, and we have the responsibility to care for them.

Just as mothers let nothing stand in the way of protecting their infants, we will not let anything interfere with our protecting our body from harm. And just as mothers take great pride in keeping their infants healthy, we can take pride in keeping our body healthy.

Insult and Injury

Blame has no place in recovery.

If we recognize addiction as a disease, we turn our attention to recovery and avoid blaming ourselves or others. It is equally important that codependents stop blaming themselves or others for their dependency, and realize that being codependent is not being bad.

The wife of a man who had completed a course of treatment complained that whenever she said or did something, he would say, "You're acting like a codependent!" She felt that in recovery he had picked up a new tool to use against her.

This woman had not bothered to find out what a codependent is, and reacted as though it were a four-letter word. A simple way to view this is that the addict plays the tune and the codependent dances to it. Recovery from codependency means giving direction to your own life instead of constantly reacting to someone else's behavior.

If the wife had not viewed codependency as an insult, she might have responded, "You bet I am, and I am learning how to regain control over my own life."

Learning more about codependency can free you from its restrictions and discomforts.

Worthless Substitutes

Beware of worthless substitutes.

When the band of my wristwatch broke, I kept my watch in my pocket, taking it out whenever I needed to know the time. Without my watch on my wrist, I was conscious that something was missing, and this consciousness made me reach into my pocket whenever I needed to know the time.

Upon removing a rubber band from some papers, I slipped it onto my wrist. Having something on my wrist took away the missing feeling. Thereafter, whenever I wanted to know the time, I looked at a rubber band, which could not help me.

If you know you are lacking something, you can make an effort to look for it. But if you only substitute something worthless that gives you the delusion of value, then you are in trouble. The worthless substitute will offer a false sense of security, and nothing else.

If we have problems in life and face up to the fact that we have them, we can find solutions. But if we take a chemical that does nothing to solve our problems, and only distracts our attention from them, then we lose the one thing that can save us: the awareness that problems exist.

Chemicals do not solve problems, any more than a rubber band can tell time.

Fellowship or Selfishness?

There is a constructive type of selfishness.

A woman at an Al-Anon meeting once said, "They call these self-help groups, but they are not. *Self*-help is what I was doing for years before I came to these groups. I was trying to do things by myself, and I was getting sicker and sicker."

This may be more than just semantics. If these groups are self-help, the *self* is the group, not the individual. When people indulge in self-help, they get nowhere. But by becoming part of a group that tries to help itself, people become better.

Some people try self-help—even reading the Big Book and the Twelve Step literature—but they do not attend meetings. Invariably, this does not work because, as the woman said, when she tried self-help she just became sicker. It is only when we become part of the group and have the group identity that it all works.

Some people say that the Twelve Step programs are selfish. Perhaps so, but it is not a selfishness of the individual. It is a selfishness of the group—the entire fellowship—because the entire fellowship becomes the "self."

How wonderful it would be if all humanity were selfish in this way: to stop thinking of ourselves as individuals, and think of all people as one great big self. What a wonderful world such a selfishness would produce!

Spiritual Awakening

Spirituality is an effective approach to prevention.

During every administration, the president reveals strategies for overcoming the scourge of drugs, primarily by enforcing methods to make them unavailable. The fact is that, if drugs such as cocaine were eliminated, other drugs would be waiting in the wings—drugs that can easily be manufactured in amateur laboratories.

We will not win the war against drugs until we overcome the demand. People who do not feel good want to feel good. And as long as feeling good is the driving force in people's lives, people will take chemicals to get that feeling.

There is an alternate goal, which we refer to as a "spiritual awakening." This does not mean that the heavens open up with some exotic vision. Rather, we come to an awareness that there is more to life than providing our body with physical contentment or just feeling good.

People who are not religiously oriented are concerned that spirituality means becoming very religious. In my book *I'd Like to Call for Help, But I Don't Know the Number*, I point out that spirituality is not the same as religion. Finding a goal in life other than simply feeling good does not require being devoutly religious. With the alternate goal of spirituality, people are much less likely to resort to chemicals.

Sleep Without Chemicals

Healthy sleep does come eventually.

Some people in early recovery are unable to sleep. This problem can exist for some duration, particularly if you had been using tranquilizers. While insomnia can be most annoying, no one ever died from it. On the other hand, chemicals have killed many people. The tradeoff of some sleeplessness for life is a good one.

Here are a few helpful hints. Avoid *all* caffeine. Some people are sensitive to sugar, so it may be wise to reduce your sugar intake. Exercise regularly—not right before bedtime, but earlier in the day; try jogging, skipping rope, swimming, aerobics, or brisk walking. Read a book on progressive muscle relaxation. It may sound silly, but it does work. You begin by relaxing your toes and work your way up to your ears. Don't give up after the first try. Expecting instant results is part of addiction, not of recovery.

Put your clock where you can't see it from your bed. Early in recovery, some people sleep for fifteen minutes at a time. If they see the clock each time they wake up, they swear they did not sleep for even a second, because all they remember is watching the clock. Keep the Big Book at your bedside. If you can't sleep, at least you can use your time constructively.

Remember, time takes time. After bludgeoning the brain with chemicals for years, give it time to recover.

You Are Needed

You need the program, and it needs you.

Traveling in an airplane one time, I noticed all was quiet and everyone was minding his or her own business. Suddenly there was severe turbulence, and the plane was tossed about. People began talking to one another, some seasoned flyers trying to reassure the less experienced while others made light of the danger with gallows humor. The isolation that had prevailed in tranquility was replaced by group activity in time of peril.

At the treatment center, we had one session we referred to as "bus stop." A bus stop is where many people congregate, each person going his or her own way, without a common goal. This session focused on whether people in recovery are isolated individuals, or a group that can share a common goal.

When people share strength, hope, and courage, their recovery becomes easier. The more people there are at a meeting, the greater is the group support. If you can make recovery just a bit easier for someone, why not do it?

We all need meetings; if you think that you do not, you should nevertheless be there for others.

The Power of Prayer
❧

There is power in prayer.

Someone asked a theologian, "Are our prayers really heard?" He answered, "Do you listen?" In other words, prayer must be directed inward as well as outward. We ask God to hear, but we must also hear. We must listen to our own prayers. There is also an advantage in praying together. Hearing someone else's words can have greater impact than a soliloquy.

Do we really want serenity? If so, why do we do things that are likely to create turbulence rather than serenity? Do we really desire to change things? If so, why do we not use the courage that we possess? Being courageous does not rule out being lazy. A person can have courage, but just not bother to change things.

In active addiction, a person seeks the tranquility of chemical anesthesia. Some people think that sobriety should provide tranquility without chemicals. But serenity is not tranquility. Indeed, there is nothing tranquil in accepting the things that are unchangeable.

It is said that ignorance is bliss. If so, then wisdom cannot be bliss. If we pray for wisdom, we must be ready to cope with its side effects.

The Healing Power of Laughter

❦

Laughter is good for both body and soul.

Obviously there are things in life that cannot be dismissed with laughter. But there are some problems that can be minimized by making them appear ridiculous.

For example, suppose you are about to take an exam for something rather important, such as a professional license. If you fail the exam, the disappointment will be unpleasant and depressing, and you may have to wait for months before you can take the exam again. And thoughts of failure may escalate your anxiety to an intensity of panic—and in a state of panic your mind may go blank.

If you see such anxiety developing, defuse the situation by exaggerating it to the point of absurdity. Think: "If I fail the exam, they will announce it on national TV at prime time. Everyone coast to coast will know that I flunked. At the international summit they will talk of nothing else but my flunking."

Or a young woman concerned about a pimple on her forehead may think that national magazines will feature her face on the cover of their next issue, and astronauts in orbit will focus their powerful cameras on her forehead.

When you laugh at such things, you diminish their impact. AA discovered this a long time ago.

End the Stigma of Addiction
❦

We must learn to overcome the stigma of addiction.

Some people have avoided the recovery programs because they could not visualize themselves ever saying, "My name is Jane Doe, and I am an alcoholic" or "I am an addict." There is still a widespread misconception of addiction as a moral degeneracy, and people who feel this way do not wish to denigrate or incriminate themselves. They may literally choke on the words *alcoholic* or *addict*.

Here's a simple suggestion. Introduce yourself by saying, "My name is Jane Doe. I am a beautiful person with the disease of addiction."

This is a good formula for everyone. Realizing you are a beautiful person and that you have a disease is most important in recovery. Yet during active addiction, people usually are oblivious of this. Knowing that you are a beautiful person eliminates the feelings of inadequacy that make people unable to cope, leading to escape into chemicals. Knowing that you have a disease eliminates the futile attempt to control your addiction through willpower. There is no known disease that responds to willpower.

Diseases can affect everyone, even beautiful people.

Denial

There is nothing more frustrating than denial.

A compulsive gambler told me that he has just lost a good job because he passed bad checks, his fiancée broke their engagement, he's over $100,000 in debt and driving his parents into bankruptcy, and is so desperate he is contemplating suicide. When I told him that he must begin recovery by going to a rehab center, he remarked, "Do you really think my problem is that serious?"

Or consider the wife of a chief of surgery at a major hospital. She stated that when her husband comes home he sits down in front of the TV with a couple of six-packs, and that is where he wakes up the next morning. "He still makes it to the hospital every day," she said. "But any day now he will go into the operating room obviously under the influence, and then it will be all over for all of us." Yet when I suggested attending Al-Anon meetings, she said, "Oh no! Someone might see me there and think my husband has a problem, and that will affect his practice." It is as though she had never said that worse exposure was imminent.

We may never see through our own denials, even in abstinence. Our only salvation is to be as honest as we can with people in a position to help. When they point out something we do not see, give it serious consideration.

God's Role in Recovery

One of the AA traditions reads, "For our group purpose there is but one ultimate authority—a loving God."

There are numerous proofs for the existence of God, but ingenious as they are, all can be rebutted. It is possible, however, to see proof of the existence of God in the unparalleled success of AA and NA.

AA and NA are worldwide, with several million members. Can you think of any multinational corporation with even a fraction of that many employees, run without a boss? AA and NA have no authoritative management body, yet in every country there are AA and NA, and in many communities there are multiple meetings. These meet regularly, begin on time, and end on time. If we were to total the money collected in the baskets each week, it would equal the revenues of major multinational corporations. Yet no company has been able to operate as smoothly and as efficiently as AA or NA.

And what is the product of AA and NA? Keeping people sober and clean! No company—whether it manufactures automobiles or runs oil wells and refineries—faces anywhere near the challenge that AA and NA do.

There can be only one answer for why this works so well. There is one supreme authority in charge of the fellowship, and He runs the program efficiently. Obviously, He must be present at the meetings. You can find Him there if only you look for Him.

The Rewards of Discipline
🍎

We may not enjoy doing everything we are required to do in recovery.

The following is a letter from an alumnus of the treatment center.

"I'm still sober and I have you to thank. On the most glorious adventure, sailing up the Pacific Coast, I was doing okay because we pulled into port every two to four days and could find a meeting. However, the farther north we got the harder it was to find a meeting and the more I came to rely on literature. (Everyone else on board was drinking, some like raging alcoholics.)

"It became a very high-pressure situation for me. I was truly considering taking a drink, and I kept telling myself "Not right now, maybe in an hour." I went through several days of living hour to hour until I came across the book that saved my sobriety. It was the journal I had kept while I was in treatment. (I didn't even know it was in the books I had packed.) Needless to say, as I reread all my craziness and all the pain from sobering up, it broke through the denial that had sprung up and took me back to my First Step; most importantly, it took the focus off the dysfunction around me and back on my own spirituality.

"I did not like writing the journal at the time. Now I am deeply grateful that I followed your suggestions."

It is wise to do what people who are the experts tell us to do.

Preventing Relapse
❧

Relapse is an unfortunate occurrence, but may be preventable.

The difficulty of life is not "It's just one thing after another," but rather "It's the same damn thing over and over again." Listening to someone who relapsed or is approaching relapse, we hear the same kind of thinking as characterized active addiction.

A woman who is sixteen years sober thinks she can be a social drinker again. "We were the children of the sixties," she said, "That's what caused us to use drugs. Alcohol wasn't even all that much on the scene. Now I'm older and much more mature. There isn't any reason that I can't take a drink." Obviously she is forgetting how often she used to get stoned on beer. Although still abstinent at this point, her addictive thinking has recurred. Some questioning reveals that this woman has not attended a meeting for a long time.

When we first enter recovery, we recognize how distorted our thinking had been. As long as we continue active participation in the program, we are shielded against a return of the insanity of addiction. Working with newcomers is especially helpful in recognizing the treacherous nature of addictive thinking. Drifting away from the program can lead us back to the hell that we swore we would never revisit.

Becoming Truly Human

Step Six: Were entirely ready to have God remove all these defects of character.

Some people have trouble with Step Six, saying the words but thinking, "Please, God, don't take me seriously." They are like the patient who is told that she must give up indulging in food, drink, and sex. "Will I live to be 100?" she asks. "No," the doctor answers, "but it will feel like it."

Some people believe that fun in life is contingent on gratifying at least a few character defects, and that life devoid of all defects is tantamount to being a monk. This is not true. The world was given to us to enjoy—but as dignified humans, not like brute beasts.

Self-mastery for the recovering addict includes abstinence from chemicals. It also includes self-restraint in gratifying the biological drives that every human being has.

If God had desired more angels, He would have created them. He created us as physical beings with physical drives that should be gratified. But while we are not meant to be angels, neither are we meant to be animals, for God has an abundance of these also.

We are meant to be human beings, and that is spirituality.

What Next?

World leaders can learn much from Al-Anon.

When the Berlin Wall collapsed and the communist world disintegrated, an editorial asked, "What do we do next?"

This response was not novel to people familiar with chemical dependency. Marriages that survive the stress of active addiction can fall apart when the addict recovers. The spouse who had become adept at dealing with drunkenness now has no idea how to deal with sobriety. Similarly, the Free World had to learn how to relate to communism. Now that the enemy is vanquished, "What on earth do we do now if these countries become democracies?"

Perhaps if the world's political leaders would attend Al-Anon, they might learn that the answer is to get their own act together. We have poverty, alcohol- and drug-ridden youth, serious crime, and a system unable to deal with these problems. We have serious economic problems. We are not at a loss for problems of our own.

What would happen if we got our act together instead of trying to fix the rest of the world? Exactly what happens when the nonaddicted spouse makes the necessary changes in his or her own functioning: the addict begins to recover.

Life Without Fear

Fear is an element of all chemical dependencies.

The fear is not panic or agoraphobia, but a terror that has been described as follows by a recovering person: "Ever since I was a kid I felt I was walking through a minefield."

When we walk through a minefield, we are aware that the next step may blow us to bits. If the next step is survived, it may be the one after that. There is no relief, because minefields are everywhere: at home or at work, when alone or with friends. The only respite is a chemical, for the brief period of its action.

But these minefields exist only in our imagination. They are as unreal as other hallucinations. This is the insanity to which the program refers—the insanity of believing there are mines where none exist.

Some psychologists help a person walk safely through the minefield. The Twelve Step program helps a person realize that the minefields do not exist.

The promise of recovery is serenity instead of fear. Gradually the mines disappear, and we can direct our efforts to dealing with the challenges of the real world that *do* exist. With recovery we gain the wisdom to know the difference.

Acceptance

Sobriety involves coping with the challenges of reality.

In recovery, we should avoid unrealistic expectations. Many people resorted to chemicals to escape what they felt was too harsh a reality. But reality does not necessarily improve with abstinence. While chemicals complicated things and made reality more difficult, many of the stresses that were there before the chemicals are still there with abstinence.

A woman in recovery said, "They told me that when I got sober things would get better. Well, things didn't get better. *I* got better." A woman who had a child with birth defects stated, "I prayed that God would perform a miracle and change him. One day God did perform a miracle. He changed me."

A key word in recovery is *acceptance*: to accept that we have the disease of addiction and adjust ourselves to that fact, and to accept countless things that we cannot change. But it is important not to confuse acceptance with approval. Accepting something does not mean we have to be pleased with it. There is nothing wrong with telling God about our displeasure.

We may be angry at God when we are in distress, but we turn to Him for security and pray for the serenity to accept the stresses in life.

Nobody's Perfect
❦

The Twelve Step program states that the aim in recovery is progress rather than perfection.

Some people insist on achieving perfection. These are usually individuals who have unwarranted feelings of inferiority. Because they consider themselves inadequate, they have extraordinary fears of failure. To avoid the devastation of failure, they try to be perfect.

No one enjoys failing. Yet we know that life consists of both successes and failures, and all one can hope for is that our successes outnumber our failures. If we do fail, we are understandably upset, but we do not lose it all together. Failures are unpleasant, but they are not catastrophes.

Insisting on perfection always backfires. In trying to cover every conceivable detail that might possibly go wrong, we exhaust ourselves, and the job doesn't get done.

If we get to know our real selves, we will not have these feelings of inadequacy. We will then be able to adjust to reality by enjoying our successes and surviving our failures.

The Worst Failure Is the Failure to Try

Doing nothing is the greatest failure of all.

Yesterday we discussed the futility of trying to avoid failure by being absolutely perfect. Another way of avoiding failure is to do nothing. If we pull the covers over our head and stay in bed until 4 P.M., there is little we can do that can go wrong. To some people, passive failure is more acceptable than active failure.

If we cannot control the outcome of events, we are not at fault if we fail. But since we *do* control whether or not we try to do something, we are at fault when we do not try.

Recovery from addiction is a major step at trying. As we gain confidence in ourself, we are progressively encouraged to advance further. Coping, trying, and recovery go hand-in-hand.

Be Open to Spiritual Awakening
❦

In recovery we refer to a "spiritual awakening."

A young man described a life of drugs that had resulted in crazy highs and close brushes with death. He related that his girl friend had overdosed, and as he frantically tried to revive her, he prayed, "Please God, don't let her die." When she began to breathe, he felt God had answered his prayers. "I felt I was touched by God's spirit." Yet his drug use continued unabated.

When he ran afoul of drug dealers, he was a target of a gangland murder attempt. He still has the bullet at the base of his skull. He remembers thinking as he was hit, "Oh God, please save me," and again he felt touched by the spirit of God. Yet he continued to use drugs as before.

Twice this man had a spiritual experience, and twice it did not change his way of living. Why? Because these experiences were spiritual *awakenings*. When the alarm clock buzzes, we have the option of getting up or of shutting off the alarm and going back to sleep. Awakening is only an option—an opportunity. We must make a choice whether to get up or to go back to sleep.

Likewise, a spiritual awakening is an arousal, which we can take as a starting point for a new way of living, or ignore and go back to our old ways. The good judgment is to take advantage of the awakening.

Don't Isolate Yourself

Defense mechanisms are not always benign.

Some of our body's defense mechanisms can cause more harm than good. For example, if we have a joint inflamed, the body heals the inflammation by forming scar tissue, but this scar tissue immobilizes the joint, so that the healing process causes the deformity of arthritis.

The same is true of our emotional defenses. If we are sensitive and afraid of being hurt by others, we will defensively isolate and withdraw—other people can't hurt us if we avoid them. But this avoidance results in a loneliness that is even more painful.

We have to undo the defense mechanisms that back-fire. Doctors prescribe medications to prevent scar-tissue formation. Similarly, when we feel ourselves withdrawing and isolating, we must make a deliberate and conscious effort to relate to other people. While we all crave companionship, some of us may be too frightened to have it.

Belonging to a recovery fellowship can be advantageous, because the empathic and loving support of the group allows us to emerge from our isolation in a protective environment.

Self-Pity is Often a Waste of Time
❦

Sometimes we focus excessively on pain.

If you have a sore spot in your mouth, you are likely to keep feeling that spot with your tongue. Something about pain attracts us to keep in contact with it. Much the same happens with emotional pain. We revisit painful incidents in our minds. Even though it hurts each time we think of them, we relive the painful episodes.

But ruminating about painful incidents uses up both time and energy that could be directed toward constructive activities. This rumination is not only useless, because we cannot undo the past, but gives rise to resentments against those we think were responsible for hurting us.

Dwelling on painful experiences is detrimental for everyone, but particularly dangerous for people in recovery. In the program, this is referred to as a "pity party," and if we do not discontinue it, we are prone to relapse. We may use the idea, "I hurt so bad and no one understands" as justification for drinking or using chemicals.

What can we do about this tendency to focus on pain? We can try as hard as we can to overcome it, which makes us ready to have God remove it, if only we ask Him sincerely to do so.

Everyone Can Learn from the Twelve Steps
❦

The real difference between addicts and nonaddicts is that the former use chemicals and the latter do not.

That is, the struggles and emotional problems addicts face are really no different from those experienced by anyone else. It also means that the people who help the chemically dependent person cope are probably capable of helping others as well.

Bill Wilson, cofounder of AA, said, "How to translate a right mental condition into a right emotional resolve, and so into easy, happy, and good living, is the problem of life itself."

Psychologists say that life becomes problematic when there is a lack of harmony between cognition and affect, or between ideas and feelings. Same thing.

A person with a phobia of crowds logically knows that there is nothing really dangerous there, but nevertheless has anxiety or panic as though something terrible were about to happen. These symptoms are a result of emotions, not logic.

In *Waking Up Just in Time*, I use the "Peanuts" comic strip to demonstrate how the Twelve Steps of AA are excellent guidelines for nonaddicts as well.

Not All Conflict is Bad

Friction is essential for growth.

Our daily lives involve mechanical things, so we tend to apply engineering principles to our personal lives and behavior. For instance, we lubricate our automobile engines and appliances to enhance their performance, because friction is bad for a machine.

So, too, we try to minimize emotional friction. But friction is necessary for growth and development. In fact, much of growth depends on overcoming challenges. Not all conflict should be avoided.

If you assist your children with their homework by helping them understand the teacher's instructions so that they can do the work, this is constructive. If you do the homework for them and remove the challenge, they learn nothing.

Addiction is often the result of trying to make things run friction-free via chemicals. We ease ourselves into sleep with chemicals, and we ease ourselves out of tension with chemicals. Indeed, some people talk of "lubricating" themselves with alcohol.

When we eliminate mind-altering drugs, we restore the healthy friction necessary for our growth. The recovery program shows us how to make friction constructive.

Don't Be So Hard on Yourself

The poet Goethe said of someone, "He is a man whom it is impossible to please, because he is never pleased with himself."

Some people adjust to life fairly well. While they may not always be happy, they are able to cope even when they experience distress. Others are not only unable to adjust to distress but also cannot tolerate life when nothing is wrong.

When we are pleased with ourselves, we do not become extremely displeased, even when things go awry. But if we are displeased with ourself, nothing is ever satisfactory. Efforts to please are attempts to fill a bottomless pit.

A person who is chronically displeased is vulnerable to alcoholism or drug addiction. Unless the source of this displeasure is removed, the chemical dependency will only be replaced by excessive food, money, or sex.

Constant displeasure is a problem of low self-esteem. When our self-image is poor, we are displeased with ourselves. But working the Twelve Steps can help us avoid the bottomless pit.

Let's assume that you are sober. Do you still feel displeased much of the time? If so, think about what Goethe said, and begin doing things that will enable you to be pleased with yourself.

Workaholism

Workaholics have a problem with self-esteem.

Some people with low self-esteem think of themselves as inadequate in every way. Others feel adequate insofar as their work is concerned, but consider themselves inadequate in other ways.

Professional people, for example, may think themselves competent as doctors, lawyers, or nurses but otherwise uninteresting or undesirable. The hospital or office becomes a comfortable place, whereas the home or social gatherings are places where they feel ill at ease. They may become workaholics because the workplace is where they feel the best.

Some people say, "I never take a drop at the office. I only drink at home." This is almost invariably a sign of the need for anesthesia at home, where they must be a social person rather than a professional.

Self-awareness can eliminate this negative view of oneself as only half a person.

Life is an Adventure

Life can be exciting.

A great actress was excited on the last day of an extended run on Broadway. That day, she had thought of a new way to act the part. Her co-actors said, "But this is the last day. The play has run its course." Her enthusiasm was not dampened. "There is still today." The actress was excited about the one remaining performance as though there were to be a thousand more.

This is the attitude that develops from living one day at a time. True, we cannot change the past, nor is there much that can be done about the future. But today is what really counts. When infants begin to crawl, they explore their environment looking for new things. Not burdened by the past or contemplating the future, they howl with glee at every new discovery.

The past may weigh on our minds, and we tend to worry about the future. If only we could relieve ourselves of these burdens, we would be like the infant, enjoying every new thing.

There are so many things to discover in life. Living one day at a time can help us make those discoveries.

You Can Survive Relapse

While relapse is unfortunate, it is not a calamity.

One winter day as I walked to the post office, I tried to avoid the icy spots on the sidewalk. Halfway there, I slipped and sustained some bruises. But I arose and continued toward my destination, walking much more carefully.

As painful as the fall was, I was nevertheless closer to my destination. The fall did not put me back to the starting point. And because I sustained some bruises, the slip made me more cautious. Had I not fallen earlier, perhaps I would not have been as cautious, and a later slip might have been more dangerous.

Relapse should be looked at this way. The growth achieved prior to the relapse is not undone, and the extra caution after the relapse can prevent a greater disaster.

I would certainly have preferred to avoid the fall, but once it happened, I could consider how it benefited me. The same is true of relapse.

Don't Allow Fear of Religion to Keep You From Recovery

❧

The Twelve Step program advocates reliance on a Higher Power.

A recently developed recovery program criticizes AA and NA as too God oriented and as fostering excessive dependency. Its advocates claim that this discourages people from recovery.

Most addicts are discouraged by the AA and NA concept of absolute abstinence rather than by its philosophy. If a program advocated social drinking or recreational use, they would flock to it even if it were steeped in religious ritual.

Some religiously devout people shun the Twelve Step program, while some avowed atheists follow it. No one in the program asks for evidence of attendance at church or synagogue. We choose anything or anyone we wish to serve as our Higher Power.

Only time will reveal the effectiveness of this new approach. Since addiction is life-threatening, we should be cautious about unproven programs and view them in comparison to the one with more than a half-century track record.

Share Your Feelings With Others
❦

Feelings that are shared can be tolerated.

Marilyn is a fifty-seven-year-old widow who cared for her two grandchildren while her daughter went to work. One night Marilyn felt chest pain and shortness of breath. After three days of intensive tests, her doctor told her, "There is nothing wrong with you." Her daughter was thrilled, but was surprised at Marilyn's crying. "Why are you crying, Mom? You're okay! No heart attack!"

The day before the chest pain, the daughter had become engaged to be married. Her fiancé had been promoted at work, and was relocating to a distant city. Marilyn was supposed to be happy for her daughter, but what would she now do with herself? There would be no one to cook for, no one's laundry to do, no one to look after.

Marilyn felt she was being deserted by those she loved, but could not allow herself to be angry at her daughter's good fortune. The anger that she refused to admit had tightened her chest muscles to cause pain and shortness of breath. While Marilyn did not have a heart *attack*, she did have heart*ache*, and no one to share it with.

The recovery program enables us to share our feelings, which eliminates the need for chemicals as well as chest pain.

Trust in a Higher Power
🍎

The Higher Power may override our better judgment.

One day a man approached me. "I am Evelyn's husband," he said. "She is twelve years sober," and he showed me a family picture taken at their twenty-fifth wedding anniversary.

I remembered Evelyn. Many admissions to detox, three rehabs, six months in a halfway house, all followed by relapse. "The last time I spoke to you," the man said, "it was 1:00 A.M., in a phone call from the emergency room. They refused to admit Evelyn, and you prevailed upon them to admit her. That was her last detox, and she has been sober since."

I wish I could take credit for that decision. After so many relapses, my judgment would have been to stop enabling by rescuing her again. Somehow my better judgment did not prevail, and a Higher Power directed me to authorize the admission.

It is wonderful that the Higher Power often steps in when our own judgment, which may seem so infallible, is inadequate.

Depression

Recovering people are susceptible to the same diseases as nonaddicts.

Some people have a depressive outlook on life. Some people become depressed when they sustain a loss. And some people are depressed when they must give up their chemicals. But there is also a kind of depression that results from certain chemical changes in the body, that can occur in addicts and nonaddicts alike.

This latter type of depression can be treated with safe, nonaddictive antidepressants. The failure to treat such depression can result in prolonged dysfunction, severe suffering, and even suicide.

A recovering person with severe depression should be evaluated by someone competent in the diagnosis of dual disorders. While addicts are prone to take medication indiscriminately, they should not be deprived of nonaddictive medication that can be life-saving.

Recovering people who need medical treatment for depression should not be excluded from the program and deprived of the support the fellowship can provide when that need is greatest.

A Dialogue With God

Turning our lives over to the will of *God as we understand Him* warrants clarification.

At the risk of being accused of sacrilege, I present a fantasied dialogue between an addict and God:

"Okay God, I give up. My life is a mess. Help me out of this," the addict exclaims.

"Of course I will help you. But first you must discontinue messing things up," is the Divine response, "otherwise it is like trying to bail out a boat when the water is coming in faster than you can get it out."

"But I'm not drinking or drugging any more, God. What else do you want me to do?"

"Make a list of everything you have done," says God, "then get someone to help you discover what parts of your behavior are constructive and which are destructive. Then I want you to compensate others for any harm you have done to them and ask their forgiveness. Be on the alert for repetition of any destructive behavior, and if it occurs, don't defend it. Then come back to Me and I will help."

Until we have done this, our character defects are likely to influence our thinking and we may conclude that the will of God is what *we* want. We can arrive at what is truly God's will only if we eliminate the personal interests that are the products of our character defects.

The Dialogue Continues
🍎

The dialogue between the addict and God continues:

"But God, I'm in trouble now, deep trouble," the addict pleads. "I need help now. I can't wait for Your help until I correct my character defects."

"You never were able to wait, were you?" responds the Divine One. "Wanting a quick fix is a character defect you must get rid of. You just begin working on changing yourself and on correcting character defects, and I'll help you. But no bargaining or trading. Your efforts at self-improvement must be sincere."

"Okay I'll begin," promises the addict. "But what's in it for me, God? What do I get out of all of this?"

"What's in it for you?" God responds. "You had said you were willing to do *My* will. The question should be 'What is it that God wants?' rather than 'What's in it for me?'"

"Okay. What is it that you want from me, God?"

"It's simple," God says. "I sent the message through Micah 6:8: 'What is it that God asks of you, but to do justice, love benevolence, and walk humbly with your God.'"

"Is that all there is to it, God? I thought it was much more complicated."

"No, my child, it is not at all complicated. Keep it simple."

There Are No Short Cuts to Recovery
🐛

Patience helps us develop real goals.

Someone said that a shortcut is often the quickest way to some place you don't want to be. Virtually every use of chemicals is a quick fix. While chemicals certainly do not fix anything, there is no denying that they are quick. But where do you go so quickly? Nowhere, if you are lucky. If you are not lucky, you go someplace you really don't want to be.

Some people risk their lives by reckless speeding. Even when there is no imminent danger, we may become so infatuated with speed that we lose sight of the fact that we have no ultimate goal.

The recovery program teaches that "time takes time." When we rid ourselves of an obsession with speed, we can focus on where we are going. Only then can we discover our goals as well as the means of achieving them.

Sharing the Wisdom of the Program
🐛

Is life nothing more than addictions?

Some people say that the proliferation of addictive diseases and treatment programs has made the term *addiction* meaningless. The extension of the Twelve Step program from alcohol to drugs, gambling, sex, smoking, excessive spending and eating, as well as the development of the concept of codependence, has put virtually everyone in the category of either addict or codependent.

Let's keep things simple. If addiction is defined as a detrimental behavior in which people persist because they are unable to stop doing it, then whatever falls under that definition is addiction, whether it applies to one person or millions. In times of epidemics, when an entire community has a particular disease, it would make no sense to say people were not sick because everyone was sick. If we find that we are doing something self-destructive, and we would rather not do this thing yet are unable to stop, then this is addiction.

The Twelve Step program begins with the realization that, if we are unable to control a destructive behavior, we must enlist some source of strength to help us. The rest of the steps are an effective method to accomplish this. Finally, we share a statement of responsibility that we have found a successful method to save our lives.

When Fear Is Legitimate

Not all fears are bad.

A man with five years of recovery complained that the program was not working because he was still full of fear. "How do you ever get to feel safe?" he asked. Apparently he was confusing two distinct types of fear: unhealthy and healthy.

Unhealthy fear is the anxiety resulting from anticipating that something is going to go wrong, and nothing can be done to avoid it. This fear has no basis in reality when there is no reason to anticipate something terrible. This fear is alleviated by working the Twelve Steps and turning over to Got those things beyond your control.

There is also a healthy fear that we may drink or use chemicals again, which has a logical basis because we were once a victim of such compulsion. The fear keeps us from becoming overconfident and drifting away from the program. We may never be completely safe from relapse, but we can do something to help avoid it: stay in contact with the program.

You can't prevent a tornado, so don't worry about one. You *can* prevent relapse, so take precautions to avoid it.

The Rewards of Meditation

Step Eleven refers to prayer and meditation.

We know what it means to pray, but how many of us meditate? Furthermore, what is meditation anyway?

To meditate means to eliminate all other thoughts from your mind and concentrate all thinking on a single subject. You can meditate about the seams on a baseball or about the wings of a mosquito. While that would be silly meditation, it is meditation nevertheless.

Once we have decided to turn our life over to the will of God as we understand Him, it is important that these not be just pleasant-sounding words, devoid of meaning. If we are sincere, we must truly set aside time to think seriously about what the will of God is.

Meditation is not easy. If we concentrate on the will of God, our thoughts will roam every which way: our job, vacation, sports, the economy. It takes a concerted effort to bring ourselves to meditating. That is because meditation can be uncomfortable. It means committing ourselves to do what God wants instead of what *we* want.

If we wish to fully develop our character, we must make that commitment. Take a few minutes out of your busy schedule to meditate. You will find it most rewarding.

A Model for Life
❦

Table tennis can be a model for life.

Behavior consists of action and reaction. Sometimes we initiate action, and other times we react to what someone else does. In the addicted family, both action and reaction become grossly distorted.

In playing Ping-Pong, when I serve I direct the ball where I want it to go, with whatever force I choose. After five serves, I surrender this advantage to the other player. When he hits the ball to me, I return it as effectively as possible, but now I am *re*acting. Those are the rules of the game.

In the addicted family, people do not abide by the rules. Some people always want to serve, and others always want to react. This is the pattern in codependence, when the addict claims all the serves and the codependent only reacts.

We have control over our serves, but not how the other player responds. In the addicted family, some people think that they control not only what *they* do but also the other person's response, and they are frustrated when the other person does not react the way they wish.

In real life we need to analyze whether we are serving or returning the serve. We need to be aware that, regardless of how we hit the ball, we can never control how the other person is going to return it.

Accept Yourself and You'll Accept Others

How we relate to others depends greatly on how we feel about ourselves.

If we react to character defects in ourselves by realizing that they are part of our human makeup, and that we need to improve upon them, we are likely to give others this same consideration. If we condemn ourselves for every fault, we are likely to be hypercritical of others.

If we think of ourselves as likable, we are not apt to become jealous. When we think badly of ourselves, we may feel that our spouses are looking elsewhere. After all, how could they possibly be satisfied with our meager companionship and love?

If we think poorly of ourselves, we expect people to reject us, and we will avoid this rejection by isolating ourselves. Or if we believe rejection is inevitable, we avoid the suspense by precipitating the rejection.

These are just a few examples of how we can be hostile and behave badly toward others because we don't like ourselves. By improving our self-esteem we discover that we not only like ourselves more but that we like other people much more than we had thought.

Growing with Pain
❦

Pain has its redeeming features.

If we had been asked to design the world, we would certainly have eliminated all suffering. But no one asked our opinion, so we must accept reality as it is. And pain and suffering are part of reality.

Our option is how to react to that pain. We can be bitter and angry, resentful toward everyone including God. Or we can say, "What is there that I can learn from this?" The first reaction gets us nowhere, except into a doctor's office or chemically dependent. The second reaction makes us wiser. We can at least avoid some situations we know will result in distress.

One positive aspect of pain is that it can bind us together. If we hurt, we can understand that others hurt and empathize with them. We know that our pain can be eased when someone gives us a helping hand. And we can extend that help to others. Pain sensitizes us to other people; this is what makes humanity a family instead of a herd.

We pray to God to spare us from pain, but if it should occur, let us not waste the precious experience. We learn from it, seek help, accept help, and give help. That is how we grow.

Secrets Can Be a Burden

Unloading our secrets can be a relief.

It has been said that we are only as sick as the secrets we keep. If we are fortunate enough to discover that our attitudes and behavior are sick, and we look for the sources of our sickness, we are likely to discover our secrets are part of the problem.

Help from a professional therapist may be necessary if the secrets are hidden even from ourselves. But there are secrets that we do know about, which do not require a professional therapist. These are things we can share with another. Sometimes, however, we are so ashamed of them that we are reluctant to reveal them to anyone.

This is where the Twelve Step program is so helpful. When we attend meetings, we invariably hear someone share the secrets we thought were unique to us. We also find people who listen and identify with us. We can unburden ourselves so we feel so much lighter, having rid ourselves of a heavy burden. We also have more available energy, since we no longer waste energy keeping the secrets bottled up inside us.

Barriers to Intimacy

Love is the union of two lonelinesses.

Thousands of stories, poems, and songs have been written about love, yet the precise nature of love still escapes us.

When people say that they love a particular delicacy, they are not really referring to love. We do unite with the food we eat, but it is not a union of two lonelinesses. However, the love of one person for another is a union of two lonelinesses.

Why do some love relationships deteriorate? Those that were based on sexual infatuation were never love relationships to begin with. But what about loves where two people appeared to provide for each other's needs?

Your loneliness cannot be relieved by another person, no matter how much you try, unless *you let that other person into your life*. If you remain secretive and prevent the other person from knowing you, then you obstruct love. The most common reason for not letting another person get to know us is the fear that this will repel them. If we think poorly of ourselves, we set up barriers to intimacy that prevent others from loving us.

It is only when we are at peace with ourselves that we allow the closeness that can relieve our loneliness. If we feel a lack of reciprocity, we may not be allowing the other person to love us.

Self-Esteem is a Powerful Force
🍒

How we react to criticism depends on our self-image.

An alumnus from our treatment center called hysterically one day because her husband had been verbally abusive, berating her as a failed wife and mother.

After the woman calmed down a bit, I said to her, "That scar on the right of your face is absolutely ugly!"

"I don't understand you, doctor," she said.

"What is there not to understand?" I said.

"I don't have any scar on my face," the woman said.

"Then what did you think when I made that remark?" I asked.

"I hadn't the slightest idea what you were talking about," the woman answered. I pointed out to the woman that when I made an unkind remark which she knew to be untrue, her reaction was that there must be something wrong with *me*. The reason she reacted so intensely when her husband made a derogatory comment was because she believed his comments to be true. Had she thought of herself as a good wife and mother, her reaction would have been, "I don't know what in the world you are talking about." It would hardly have been the hysterical reaction she had.

If we think well of ourselves, even insulting comments, while not pleasant, can be shrugged off.

God Does Not Abandon Us
❦

The writer Lewis Carroll once said, "Everything's got a moral, if you can only find it."

We are most likely to find things only when we look for them. This applies to program meetings as well. We can learn something from every meeting, if we only look for it.

I once attended an AA meeting when I was very depressed. This was a "gratitude meeting," at which a number of people expressed how grateful they were for the wonderful things that had happened to them since they became sober. I was not in a grateful mood, and was rather irritated by all the testimonials of how wonderful life is.

The last person who spoke said, "I have been sober for four years. I wish I could tell you that it was all good. I have lost my job, my wife has sued for divorce, my car has been repossessed, and my house is up for sheriff's sale. But I don't think that God has brought me all this way only to walk out on me now."

Whereas much of the meeting seemed irrelevant to me that evening, this person said what I needed to hear in my state of mind. No matter how difficult things get, it is foolish to assume that, after helping us along so far, God is going to abandon us now.

Quitting Is Not An Option
❦

The dependence advocated by the Twelve Step program is not an unhealthy one.

A dear friend remarked to me, "The problem with Humpty-Dumpty was not that he was so fragile, but that he depended on all the king's horses and men to put him together."

Some people criticize the Twelve Step program because it fosters dependence instead of stimulating self-sufficiency. "People seem to be expecting either God or other people to help them stay sober." But this view can come only from someone who does not understand the program.

The Humpty-Dumpty rhyme tells us that if you depend on others to do everything, you can *never* get put back together again. The fact that so many people have recovered by virtue of the Twelve Step program indicates that it does not negate responsibility. We must exert maximum effort—nothing less will do. It is only after our own resources are exhausted that we can ask and receive help from our Higher Power and colleagues. To those who are critical of this approach I ask, "What would you recommend we do when all our energies have been exhausted?" Quitting is not a viable option.

Your Success Sets An Example

In recovery, just being sober can help others.

A woman said that she had been avoiding an AA meeting because the practice was to give your sobriety date each time you are introduced. With sixteen years of sobriety, she felt she was boasting. On second thought, she realized that perhaps it was good for newcomers to see people with such long sobriety.

Participation in the program is a two-way street: we give and we take. If we do not feel in need of a meeting, we should remember that our presence is evidence that there is life after sobriety.

People have told me that the reason they hadn't tried to stop drinking or using chemicals is because they were afraid they couldn't do it. They chose not to try rather than to try and fail. Each time a newcomer sees someone with long sobriety, it reinforces the fact that it *can* be done.

Most often any kind of contribution requires some action; just being somewhere does hardly any good. But this is not so when we go to a meeting. The very presence of another sober person conveys a helpful message.

No Apologies

A quality recovery requires changed habits.

I once interviewed a woman who began crying as she related some painful material, and then she said, "I'm so sorry."

"Sorry for what?" I asked.

"I'm sorry for crying," she said.

I did not understand why she was apologizing for crying, because it is reasonable to cry when one is in pain.

"I always apologize for everything I do," she said.

I advised the woman that this was an unhealthy habit. Apologies are appropriate only if we have offended someone. There is no need to efface oneself by apologizing for everything. This self-effacement is invariably the result of a low self-esteem, which should be corrected.

Upon leaving the office and seeing another patient in the waiting room, she immediately said, "I'm sorry for taking so much of the doctor's time." This was less than two minutes after she was instructed to stop apologizing. Apologizing had become a reflex action for her.

Many of our habitual behaviors are negative and should be changed. If we are not aware of them, our sponsors and trusted friends can point them out to us.

Suffering Can Bring Us Together
❦

It may be selfish of me, but I cannot agree with a recovering person who said, "I curse whoever invented these damn drugs!"

If it had not been for mind-altering chemicals, how would I ever have met and come to know so many wonderful people?

I am an avid reader, so I could have spent all my nonworking time exploring many interesting subjects. While that would have increased my knowledge, it would not have provided the emotional enrichment that comes from sharing with people in recovery. No history, philosophy, or even theology book has the warmth of a sincere hug.

The Twelve Step fellowships provide more character development than books and lectures. Nor is the opportunity to give or receive help as readily available as in the fellowships.

Coming to these experiences through chemical dependence is quite costly. Yet suffering can bring people together more than anything else. While we may wish we had never encountered the chemicals that have been so injurious, let's not forget that mutual suffering has brought us close to one another.

Don't Set Yourself Up For a Fall
❦

We learn from relapse.

A man with two months' sobriety participated in a family session, and misinterpreted something his wife said as a rejection. Upon leaving the family session he got drunk. He later stated that after having been sober for the first time in memory, he was certain nothing could make him drink again—so he was surprised at his reaction.

This incident demonstrates three important points. First, we often jump to conclusions, distorting other people's intentions. Rather than inquire what they meant, we react to what we *think* they meant. Second, even if the wife had intended rejection, reacting with drink only intensifies the rejection. Third, the overconfidence that "nothing could ever make me drink again," is the undoing of many addicts. Even people with years of quality sobriety are always at risk of relapse and need to be on guard.

Learn these three important points so you can avert costly mistakes.

Don't Let Regrets Ruin
Your Tomorrows
🍎

The principles of recovery have universal application.

A young man who had been a budding vocalist developed a throat problem. But instead of following through with the accepted treatment from a reputable surgeon, he contacted a doctor whose "miracle treatment" had been described in a magazine. Unfortunately the miracle did not work, and the vocalist remained with a disability that ruined his career. He confided that he had considered suicide several times.

While the facts vary, the problem is not an unfamiliar one. A person does something foolish, which has irreversible consequences; and he cannot forgive himself.

In one of Charles Schulz's brilliant cartoon strips, Charlie Brown explains that he cannot do anything about the future because he is "still trying to make yesterday better." Engaging in a "pity party," bemoaning the past, is a cop-out, whereby a person tries to avoid the challenges of the present and the future.

Perhaps this young man would have fared better had he become chemically dependent. Then he could benefit from the experience of the many people who have been in the same position. Instead of forever condemning themselves for what they did, these people have accepted the reality of what cannot be undone, risen above it, and gone on to live constructive lives.

Dr. Bob

Keeping it simple can be meaningful.

After delivering a lecture in Akron, Ohio, I visited Mt. Vernon, the home of Dr. Bob, founder of AA. While I was not moved by visiting Mt. Vernon, I did have an emotional experience walking into Dr. Bob's home. Some people cry.

Dr. Bob's home is a simple place, with only a few of his belongings remaining. Perhaps the only impressive things here are the clever hiding places where Dr. Bob concealed his bottles.

The man who greeted us at the door said, "Welcome home." Very few of the visitors to Dr. Bob's home live near Akron, yet this simple house where it all began is a home, a haven for all who were lost, tossed about in the deadly, stormy sea of addiction.

The grandeur of Louis XIV at Versailles is certainly more impressive, but you do not get a lump in your throat, as when you enter this very simple home.

—————————— JUNE 7 ——————————
The Lessons of Sobriety
🍎

The lessons of sobriety have wide application.

A concise statement of the philosophy of recovery is: Short-term gain with long-term risk is addictive behavior; short-term sacrifice with long-term gain is sobriety. Notice that this rule does not mention alcohol or any other chemical.

Suppose you are provoked by someone and react with fury. Invariably you later regret your behavior, and the immediate discharge of anger results in a prolonged period of painful regret. Perhaps you are overcome by an urge to buy something you cannot afford, and are then burdened with long-term indebtedness. Or you binge on sweets and then spend days trying to get rid of the weight that took just moments to acquire.

If we could feed data into a computer and print out a message that said, "Caution! This is a short-term gain and long-term loss," we might avoid much destructive behavior. In absence of such a device, we have recourse to sponsors, whom we should use wisely.

Does Society Need Recovery?
🍎

We can learn much from the recovery program.

Just as addicts rationalize their chemical use, so our society rationalizes its destructive behavior.

What can we say about a society that systematically poisons the air it breathes, pollutes its water, contaminates its soil with toxic materials, and sprays cancer-causing pesticides on its fruits and vegetables? Yet the industries that profit from these destructive acts have rationalized their actions as *beneficial* to humankind. We raze our forests, strip-mine our soil, extirpate many species of animals, and fill the sky with chemicals that threaten to convert our world into an uninhabitable hot-house—all so that people can have a "better" life. Intelligent people inhale smoke that causes cancer and emphysema, and the same government that condemns cigarettes as a leading cause of death gives bountiful subsidies to tobacco growers.

Addiction sacrifices the future for short-term gain. Our society should learn the lessons of recovery.

The Seduction of Power
❦

Power can be seductive.

A prominent attorney addressed a freshman class of law students, saying, "After sixteen years of sobriety, I know that nothing in the world can give me the sense of power that I crave the way alcohol can."

The theme of power is addressed in the first of the Twelve Steps. This man recognized his desire for power and that alcohol could give him this feeling. Reality painfully proved to him how treacherous alcohol is— that while it promises power it delivers the reverse, totally crushing him and exposing his powerlessness to the world. The attorney further recognized that alcohol remains seductive, and that the continuing promise of power can obliterate the inevitable powerlessness.

As I listened, I could not help but wonder how many of the students thought, "That may be true for him, but I am different. I can have the feeling of power without becoming powerless." How many of these young people will refuse to recognize their impotence until they are humbled by addiction?

Whoever said that alcohol was cunning, baffling, and powerful certainly knew what he was talking about.

Preventing Addiction
☙

Could the Twelve Steps be effective in preventing addiction?

School programs on prevention might adopt some of the Twelve Step principles. When children learn about the marvelous advances and science and technology, and are deeply impressed with the enormous power that humans now possess, it would be helpful to temper such teachings with an awareness that humans are still virtually powerless. As youngsters learn about the many ways in which they can control things, educators should point out that there remain some things beyond human control—such as other human beings.

Teaching these aspects of powerlessness in the school could have beneficial effects. At home, when youngsters discuss with their parents what they have learned, they can all share their ideas about powerlessness. The parents may even come to realize that ultimately they do not have control or power over their children.

At both home and at school, there would be greater emphasis on self-mastery, rather than trying to master and control everything and everyone else in the environment. This may well reduce the use of chemicals among young people.

A "Let Down" or the Next Step?
❦

A six-month alumnus of our treatment center recently complained that, although he was not drinking and things were much better both at home and at work, he nevertheless was experiencing a letdown.

During the first phase of sobriety, we can do little more than get through the day without a chemical. Habits must change and patterns of behavior that involve chemical use must be replaced with behavior conducive to abstinence. These are major changes and they are a full-time job. Only after the new life-style is stabilized can we take the next step in recovery.

During active addiction there is no chance for character building. The drive to relieve tension or for the euphoria a chemical brings supersedes all else. But with the beginning of recovery and stabilization of an abstinent life-style, the character building can begin. Rebuilding your character is at least as great a challenge as rebuilding a burned house, but the results can be even more rewarding.

When a house is afire, the flames must first be extinguished, then the charred material must be removed, and only then can we begin to rebuild. The letdown this man was experiencing is similar to the challenge of building a new structure after the ruins of the old have been cleared.

There is Nothing Wrong With Asking for Help
❦

Giving help is easier than accepting it.

A recovering woman confided to a friend that she had slept in an unheated apartment during a cold spell because the furnace repair service was backlogged several days. When friends told her that she would have been welcome in their home, she said, "I didn't want to impose on anyone."

I called this woman and expressed my regret that I would no longer ask her to help newcomers. "Please do," she said. "I am more than glad to help." I explained to her that if she was unwilling to accept help, she had no right to give it.

Perhaps asking for help is humbling, but in recovery we must learn humility. While we must avoid pathologic dependency, there are some healthy dependencies.

Polonius's famous advice was "Neither a borrower nor a lender be." When it comes to legitimate help, we can be both giver and recipient.

Recovery is a Dynamic Process
❦

Every bit of spiritual growth enhances recovery.

When I mentioned to someone that I was compiling messages for a daily inspirational book, he said, "Those are not of much value. The only people who read them are already in recovery. That's like preaching to the choir."

This is a short-sighted view of recovery. The Tenth Step requires an ongoing personal inventory, which should continue indefinitely. We are at all times vulnerable to a recurrence of character defects that we have eliminated, or even to an emergence of some new ones.

The more attention we give to issues of spirituality and character, the more likely we are to identify these defects and eliminate them.

Recovery is not a static phenomenon, and sobriety is not a steady state. Both are growth processes. While we do not claim spiritual perfection, we do aspire to spiritual progress, and reminders of spiritual concepts are always relevant.

Are Our Characters Unchanging?
❦

What are character defects and what are character traits?

Strangely enough, these may be one and the same. What we call traits or defects may depend on whether they exist in ourselves or in others.

I may think of myself as a person with firm convictions, but I might consider the same trait in someone else as obstinacy. I may think of myself as flexible, but I might view another person as spineless.

A particular trait may be commendable in one situation but reprehensible in another. If I refuse to forgive an injustice done to me, I am bearing a grudge or harboring a resentment. However, when I refuse to condone unjust treatment of others, I am championing the cause of the underdog.

Since recovery requires elimination of character defects, it becomes quite important that we are able to identify defects—not always an easy task. Our minds are clever, and we can deceive ourselves. I might feel that my honor has been offended, but instead of admitting this, I deny personal insult and claim I am acting on behalf of others who have been offended.

The only way to correctly identify a defect is to get an objective opinion from a competent person. A sponsor, counselor, or spiritual advisor can help.

Prayer and Humility

Prayer means different things to different people.

A person with six years of sobriety, who was militantly antireligious, related his anger when his sponsor told him to pray for sobriety. "I don't believe in God," he said, "and there is no one for me to pray to."

"You don't have to pray to *anyone*," he was told. "Just get down on your knees and pray."

"It seemed like the most stupid thing I ever did," he recounted. "I got down on my knees and prayed, even though I did not pray to anyone, and I continued doing this even though I absolutely did not believe in God. I was so desperate to get over my alcoholism that I was willing to do as I was told even though it appeared ridiculous.

"One day I made a discovery. Getting down on my knees was not an admission that there was a God, but a powerful way of my admitting that *I was not God*. It was a humbling maneuver, and that was what I needed.

"My alcoholic behavior was fueled by my grandiosity that I could control everything. I still am an atheist, but one thing I know for certain is that I am not God. I am a person who needs help to survive and I will accept help. That is something I could never do before."

Some Lessons Must Be Overcome

There is a folk saying, Someone who burns his tongue on hot soup will blow on cold soup.

Small children will avoid touching a cold stove if they were burned by touching the stove when it was hot. Although understandable, this response is inappropriate, because we react to a nonthreat as though it were a threat.

Some people have an increased sensitivity to treat new situations on the basis of previous experiences. They may relate that they are afraid of trying a new relationship because of the pain of a previous rejection. While they crave companionship, they are afraid of it. For these people, it is *not* better to have loved and lost than never to have loved at all.

When such reactions occur, it is important to recognize them and overcome them. The situation may contribute to chemical addiction, but even in the absence of chemical use, the result may be withdrawal, loneliness, or depression.

What We Gain From Addiction
❦

Addiction conveys important teachings.

A philosopher who recovered from chemical addiction once explained that the mistakes of addiction enhance the quest for spirituality: "Our resentments can teach us where to be forgiving; our lonely self-centeredness can teach us where to be loving; our fear can teach us when to trust; our hopelessness can teach us the necessity of the risk of hope. The barrier of our own self-will will teach us *what* to give up; the consequences of our self-will will teach us *why* to give up; the self-contradiction of our self-will will teach us *how* to give up."

Following the recovery program for sobriety constitutes growth, and this is never boring. We are always learning something new, and novelty can be exciting. Pursuing the goals of recovery makes recovery a fascinating process.

Our Image Obsession
❦

Undue emphasis on external appearance causes problems.

Our culture is obsessed with external appearances. If we were to add up all the money spent by both men and women on cosmetics, hair styling, wigs and toupees, plastic surgery, and the other things that affect our appearance, the total would probably exceed the Pentagon budget.

People who feel they are not attractive think that they cannot compete for affection or recognition. People who do feel attractive are apt to think that appearance is all they have to offer. Either way, they lose.

It is important that we do not get carried away by our ornamental value. Rather, we need to think of our internal value, of our importance as a human being. It is not what we look like, but who and what we are. These are the issues that belong to the realm of spirituality.

Recovery from chemical addiction requires attention to spiritual growth. As defined in my book *I'd Like to Call for Help, But I Don't Know the Number*, *spirituality* refers to the full development of our human capacities. These capacities include almost everything *other* than external appearance.

Keeping Life in Perspective
🌣

Not all unpleasantness can be easily dismissed.

Someone offered a two-step guide to living: "Don't sweat the small stuff. It's *all* small stuff."

This is not quite correct. It's not small stuff when you are fired from your job, your child gets hurt, your car is repossessed, you lose someone you love, or you discover that your child is on drugs. These are mighty big issues.

Even real small stuff, like a cinder in the eye, cannot be dismissed lightly. It may be a tiny particle, but in your eye it feels plenty big.

A better guide is, "You may not be able to stop the birds of sadness from flying over your head, but you don't have to let them nest in your hair." Whether it is big stuff or small stuff, we must realize that we have the capacity to cope and adjust.

We Can Always Use a Lift
🍎

People have told me that the message they heard one day (on the Dial-A-Sober-Thought telephone service) was exactly what they needed that particular day.

I began to wonder, is this all providential, or could there be some other reason? Gradually I realized that whatever authentic message we hear about recovery or spirituality is going to meet our needs for that day—or for that matter, *any* day.

Recovery is somewhat analogous to active addiction. A young man tried to be a controlled drinker, and gave his wife the keys to the liquor cabinet, saying, "You give me a drink only when I need it." The wife asked, "How am I supposed to know when you need it?" "No problem," he said. "Whenever you give it to me, I need it."

What is true of chemicals for the active addict is true of recovery material for the recovering person. There is always a need for a message that enhances self-esteem, helps shed resentments, or increases spirituality. Therefore, when you take hold of the program, much more comes along. Therefore, any thought about recovery can have a great effect.

Is Addiction Insanity?

Why do AA and NA refer to addiction as insanity?

After chemical use, we often behave destructively toward ourselves and others; and the aftermath is invariably misery, both physical and emotional. We frequently say, "Never again," yet the pattern recurs. Is this anything other than insane?

It is important to conceptualize addiction as insanity. If we know that we are prone to episodes of insanity, we will make a maximum effort to prevent such episodes. We cannot rely on using good judgment when such an episode recurs; in a state of insanity, we do not have good judgment to use. How absurd to say, "Next time I go insane, I'll avoid doing anything irrational."

Some physical diseases can be prevented by immunization or medication. Relapse of addiction is prevented by remaining involved in the recovery program. Delaying your program participation until you have relapsed is foolish.

Character Growth and Sobriety
🍃

There is much research underway into brain activity.

It is possible that scientists will soon discover the mechanism for our craving for chemicals. They may also develop the medications to eliminate this craving. Will there then no longer be a need for attending AA or NA meetings?

Let us look at the "dry drunk" syndrome: a person who has not had a chemical for years and does not crave, but is anything but emotionally well adjusted, manifesting all behavioral symptoms of the active addict except for using or craving. The latter are only two of the symptoms of addiction.

If medical science finds an effective way to prevent intoxication, we may think we no longer have a problem, and will not seek help from a recovery program. If the research is successful, we may indeed have fewer instances of drunk driving and disorderly conduct. But we may well have many more dry drunks, or people who think they are perfectly healthy.

The character defects of addiction can exist in abstinence of chemical use. Thus, the recovery program is necessary to enable us to make a better adjustment to life. Even with abstinence, we should continue the recovery program to ensure our character development and spiritual growth.

You Can't Control the Future
☙

What place does planning for the future have in recovery?

Someone said: "We shall surely suffer if we cast the whole idea of planning for tomorrow into a fastidious idea of providence. God's real providence has endowed us human beings with a considerable capability for foresight, and He evidently expects us to use it. Of course, we may often miscalculate the future in whole or in part, but that is better than to refuse to think at all."

Is it possible that the originator of this thought never heard of "one day at a time"? This is a quote from Bill Wilson, who had a better grasp of the program than most people do.

Failure to plan for the future is irresponsible, but there is a difference between planning for the future and trying to control the future. In active addiction we ignore the future, with an "I don't give a damn" attitude. In sobriety, we do whatever we can to the best of our ability, and *then* turn things over to a Higher Power.

No One Owes Us Anything

Is feeling hurt always a "pity party"?

Feeling sorry for ourselves may be justified. The point is that we should not get stuck in a "pity party" because, like quicksand, it can drag us down. No matter how bad things may be, failure to end a "pity party" will only make bad things worse.

We may think, "The world has been unkind to me. It now must compensate me for my suffering." We may then wait for good luck to come knocking at the door, and be very angry at the world for not delivering what we think we deserve.

No one owes you anything. If your home was blown away by a tornado, that is no one's fault. Fortunately, many people pitch in during times of misfortune, but they don't owe it to you. If they don't fulfill your expectations, you have no right to be resentful.

Feeling hurt is understandable, but we must move on in life.

Futile Gestures

Recovery teaches us to avoid futile reactions.

When I was taking driving lessons, the car in front of me abruptly stopped, and I screamed. The instructor, who was able to maintain calm under stress, said softly, "If you think screaming will stop this car, go right ahead. My suggestion is that you apply the brakes."

I think of his words often. What good could my screaming have done? Had I relied on screaming, I would have hit the car, possibly injuring myself and others. As a learning driver, I had not yet adopted the correct response of applying the brakes.

This is similar to taking a chemical in response to stress. It is not only futile but, if we allow it to substitute for the correct reaction, will bring negative consequences—similar to my screaming in order to stop the car.

Recovering people have learned to avoid useless reflex responses, and to do whatever it takes to get the job done. This is why the most efficient physicians, nurses, attorneys, laborers, and homemakers often are recovering persons. As we dispense with futile attempts to solve problems by chemicals, we also discard other ineffective responses.

The Power of Empathy

Good manners can make liars out of us.

It is rude not to say, "How are you?" upon meeting someone. We therefore ask the question, but we certainly do not wish to hear the answer.

When I meet a person in recovery who says, "How are you?" I may say, "If you have a few minutes, I'll tell you." Without exception, that person makes some time for me—not by an appointment two weeks later but right there and then, when I need it most. Does anyone know where else such instant service is available, and with such sincere interest?

People who wish to relieve themselves of an emotional burden often will engage the services of a professional. They pay to have someone listen empathetically. In the recovery program we get this service free.

Well, not completely free, because we have to return the favor. How wonderful to have a psychological barter system.

Make a Gift to God
🍎

Helping others is important to maintaining sobriety.

At a recent meeting, the speaker told of the miracle of his recovery. Some of his friends had died in addiction, and he saw his survival as a gift from God. He said, "My sobriety is God's gift to me, and when I work with newcomers, that is my gift to God. I hope that God appreciates my gift as much as I appreciate His gift to me."

Does it make any sense to give anything to God? Since He is master of the entire universe, what need could He possibly have of any gift from us?

This may sound simplistic, but we do refer to God as our heavenly Father. We can understand that an affluent father, who can get anything he wants, will still be thrilled by a gift he receives from his child; it will mean more to him than if he had bought the item himself. Why can't we think of God as being pleased with what we do for Him and enjoying the gifts of His children?

Furthermore, the importance of giving something to God is the effect it has upon us—an expression of gratitude and an indication of how much we value our sobriety.

You Cannot Force a First Step
❦

Patience is a great virtue.

As a result of better awareness, outreach, and employee assistance programs, many more young people are coming to receive help for chemical problems than in the past.

Years ago, people came for help when they hit rock bottom. The person was then ready for help, willing to surrender, fully aware that life had become unmanageable. Today's young people may not have experienced the consequences of more advanced addiction, and the idea of surrender is alien to them. They are likely to insist that they can still drink or use chemicals recreationally.

People familiar with addiction understand this attitude. If we try to force a First Step upon these young people with the insistence that they admit unmanageability, we are likely to get nothing but fierce resistance.

The realization that "half measures avail us nothing," can come only from experience. We can say, "I know exactly how you feel. That is exactly the way I felt in my early days, fully convinced that I knew what was best for me." Be just a bit more patient and allow the individual to come to his or her own realization about unmanageability. This is more likely to keep the young person coming back to meetings. In this way, denial is likely to erode and acceptance likely to occur.

Can You Become a New Person?

❦

Twenty years ago, a speaker began his talk by saying, "The man I was drank; the man I was will drink again." Abstinence from chemicals without a change in character leads to use of chemicals again.

Some people express the anxiety that sobriety will result in a new personality. "What is this new personality going to be like? How will I adjust to being a new person? How will my spouse adjust to this new person?" Observing successful recoveries in AA or NA, Al-Anon or Nar-Anon, can provide reassurance.

A miraculous transformation occurs when a lowly caterpillar spins a cocoon and later a graceful butterfly emerges. The transformation of a chemically dependent person into a sober person is no less miraculous.

I recently had the pleasure of attending the fortieth anniversary of sobriety for the speaker mentioned above. He indeed has undergone a miraculous transformation.

Real Change Requires Real Change
❦

At one meeting, a young woman who was ten days abstinent stated that she dreaded the thought of relapse. Her last ten days had been "super." However, she was under constant pressure to drink because there is drinking at her job, her friends drink, and there is drinking at all social functions. She did not want to give any of these up.

This young woman did not have her priorities in order. We who say that you must change "people, places, and things" are not being sadistic. We are simply conveying the accumulated experience that, if you do not eliminate the factors that are conducive to drinking, your risk of relapse is great. We make sacrifices when we realize that life is at stake. If you are reluctant to make changes to avoid a relapse, it is only because you have not realized how lethal addiction is.

We must learn to put first things first.

Doing the Right Thing
🍎

We must be able to take the consequences of doing what is right.

A minister who had participated in an unsuccessful intervention was upset because the irate subject left the parish for another church.

When an intervention fails, every participant is affected. It is a mistake, however, to consider refusal of treatment as a failure. An intervention weakens the person's denial and hastens the point at which he or she will eventually accept help.

Clergy should not expect their efforts to be immediately rewarded. The prophets of the Scriptures suffered persecution when they reprimanded people. So, too, parents who refuse their children's requests for sweets before a meal will be temporarily disliked. When children mature, they understand that their parents acted on their behalf.

Many addicts who were initially resentful of an intervention were later grateful that people were sufficiently concerned about them to try to stop their self-destruction.

The Journey of Life
❦

There is a beautiful prayer known as Prayer of the Traveler:

"May it be Thy will to lead me in my journey and to my destination in peace. Guide me from enemies and ambush, and all evil happenings."

When we undertake a journey, we have a goal. If we think of life as a journey with a goal, our lives will be much more orderly. We are more likely to think, "What do I want to do with my life? How am I going to get there?" We sometimes do things that don't get us anywhere because we are drifting, with no thought to our goal.

We should set goals for each day. What is it that we plan to achieve today? After the day is over, we can look to see whether we achieved our goal. If not, why not?

In our travels through life, there are enemies that lie in ambush. Among these are chemicals that can rob us of everything we hold dear. If we had to travel through enemy-infested territory, we would arm ourselves. That is precisely what we must do against the chemical enemies, which are so cunning, baffling, and powerful. One way to protect ourselves is to stay close to other people in recovery.

Recovering, Not Recovered

We can learn many things from nature.

In 1991, Mt. Pinatubo, a volcano in the Philippines, erupted with great violence after having been inactive for 600 years. The U.S. government felt secure that the volcano was extinct, and had invested billions of dollars in Navy and Air Force bases nearby.

Just as there is no security with a volcano even after many years of silence, neither is there certainty about sobriety, even after many years of abstinence. An eruption can occur with great violence, after years of being dormant.

This is why people in recovery speak of themselves as recover*ing* rather than recovered. They are aware that relapse is always a possibility, and that they must do everything to prevent such an eruption.

Break the Chains of Tyranny

Freedom is our greatest treasure.

Each July 4 we celebrate Independence Day. In every country where people have achieved independence, there is some special event to commemorate the great moment.

Being subject to someone else's domination is demeaning, particularly when the master is inconsiderate and tyrannical. We pride ourselves on having the freedom to make choices in our lives. Slavery is repulsive not only because it is cruel, but also because it is dehumanizing. Indeed, we consider freedom and humanity to be identical.

Nowhere is there a tyranny as absolute as that of chemical dependency. We become slaves to chemicals, which are the most cruel and demanding taskmasters, and rob us of every bit of freedom. When we lose our freedom to alcohol or drugs, we actually become something less than fully human.

Sobriety, therefore, means not only abstaining from chemicals but also being *freely human*. It is, of course, possible for people who are not dependent on chemicals to be slaves to their passion or their insatiable ego—which can be every bit as intoxicating as chemicals. People who are subordinate to these forces cannot be considered sober even if they abstain from chemicals.

Each day of sobriety is cause for gratitude and joy, because each day is an Independence Day.

Freedom to Choose

Choice is a right that we should never relinquish.

The psychiatrist Victor Frankl writes that when he was in the concentration camp, totally powerless and facing certain death, he maintained one choice: how to face the end of life. As crushed as he was, this remaining ability to choose gave him a dignity no one could take from him.

In addiction we lose all ability to choose because we are under the tyranny of the chemical. We do whatever the addiction dictates. Paradoxically, when we admit our powerlessness and turn our life over to the will of God, we regain the freedom to choose. How? Because the will of God is for a human being to be free—to be able to choose.

A recovering person with twenty years sobriety said, "I may drink today, but if I do, it is because I choose to do so. In my addiction, I had no choice."

As proud humans we should cherish our freedom to choose and guard it zealously.

Insatiable Drives

If what we have is not enough, more will not be enough, either.

Some of the lessons of recovery have universal application. Indeed, recovering addicts may have an advantage over nonaddicts, in that the latter may never be forced to examine their values.

The addict learns from the use of chemicals that there is never "enough." An alcoholic is someone who, upon seeing a sign ALL THE BEER YOU CAN DRINK FOR $1, orders $2 worth.

The perspective gained in quality sobriety applies to food, money, sex, acclaim, and every other human drive as well. It is said that when multibillionaire J. Paul Getty was asked, "How much money is enough?" he answered, "Just a little bit more."

Insatiable drives are destructive, regardless of what the objective is.

Keep an Open Mind
🍎

What is meant by keeping an open mind?

It is important to have convictions and not be tossed about by every new fad. In short, we do not have to agree with everyone.

It is important, however, to listen to what others have to say. *Listening* means letting other ideas enter our minds, where we can weigh them in the light of our knowledge and experience. Then we can accept all or part of them, or reject them completely.

In order for an idea to be considered, it must enter our minds. As in the physical world, two things cannot occupy the same space at one time. We must momentarily vacate our own idea in order to make room for a different idea.

As long as we know for certain "I am not an addict," the possibility that we have a chemical problem cannot even be considered. Recovery begins with an open mind.

Let Go and Let God

🍎

There are various reasons to "let go."

Generally we understand "Let go and let God" to mean that after we have done all we can do about something, we leave the rest up to God. Even just a bit of logic will reveal that there is no other option: if we have already done everything we can about something, what else is there to do except let go?

But at times there are other reasons to let go. For example, if we try very hard to fall asleep, we will remain awake and will not fall asleep until we stop trying. In other words, the only thing we can do is let go; not letting go is counterproductive.

Similarly, trying to make someone love us is virtually certain to turn the person away. It is absurd to think that we can control someone else's emotions. However, this is precisely what the active addict tries to do—and does not realize that the attempt to control everything defeats that purpose.

When we recover and let go, things begin to happen because now we are no longer being obstructive.

Be Yourself and Be Happy
❦

Just relax, and things will go better for you.

A young man told of his inability to develop a lasting romantic relationship. He had tried his utmost to impress young women, but never succeeded in attracting them. When his friend was sent to Vietnam, he asked him to take his girlfriend out occasionally for a good time while he was away. Lo and behold! She fell in love with him.

This man had a negative opinion of himself. On dates he would conceal his real self while trying to impress his companion. This facade was self-defeating, and obstructed any emotional relationship. When he entertained his buddy's girlfriend, however, he had no intention of attracting her so he did not act artificially. His real self was manifested, and the young woman fell in love with him.

Sometimes we try too hard, especially if we have feelings of inadequacy. We try to cover up something that does not need to be concealed. But if we feel good about ourselves, we can relax—and good things can happen.

Dependence on Other's Praise
🍂

Wanting to be praised is not a character defect.

A desire to hear complimentary things about ourselves is so natural that it cannot be considered a fault. Yet there are instances when we see this as an undesirable trait. What makes the difference?

If we are aware of our strengths and talents, and would like others to recognize them, there is nothing wrong with this. If, however, we need other people's compliments to let us know we are okay, then we have a problem.

In the first instance, we are aware of our reality, and we desire others to appreciate us. In the second instance, we expect others to define us because we have no self-image except what others tell us about ourselves.

Total dependence on others for our self-image is psychologically unhealthy. Doing the Fourth and Fifth Step can help achieve self-awareness, and the remainder of the Twelve Steps can help develop a personality that others can easily appreciate.

Anger at God

We are greater believers than we think.

Some people have rejected the Twelve Step recovery program on the grounds that it requires a belief in God, and they are atheists. I question the validity of some people's atheism.

A person who felt he was suffering unjustly said that he did not believe in God, and that it was therefore totally unfair for God to punish someone who doesn't believe in Him.

Reflect a moment. Is it possible to be angry at something that does not exist? Being furious with God is a profound statement of a belief in Him, and is only a strong dissent with God's sense of fairness. To say that it is unfair for God to punish someone who does not believe in His existence is a contradictory statement, evident in the confused thinking of an active addict.

God can accept our anger. We should not deceive ourselves that our anger puts Him out of existence.

Attitude and Acceptance

What must we accept, and what is subject to change?

A theologian taught his students that a person's earnings are divinely preordained for the entire year. But he also taught that a person is judged each day, and that these two statements are not contradictory.

He asked an elderly porter how he was faring, and the latter replied, "Terrible! At my age I must carry heavy burdens to earn enough to survive." A few days later he repeated the question, and the man replied, "Why complain? If at my age I still have the strength to carry heavy loads, I should be grateful."

The teacher told his students, "This man's livelihood as a porter was preordained, but his attitude varied each day." One day we may complain about our earnings and the next day be grateful that we have a job.

Even if certain facts do not change, we can always change our attitudes.

Self-Esteem and Self-Awareness

We must appreciate our self-worth.

A young addict whose arms bore many scars of heroin injections happened to be wearing a gold locket, which she had refused to sell for drugs because it had been her mother's.

I asked to see the locket, and made motions as though I were about to scratch it with a sharp instrument. "Don't do that!" the woman screamed. "That's mine, and it is very beautiful and precious to me!"

I pointed out to the woman that since she had a natural resistance to ruining something that was beautiful and valuable, the only reason she had defaced herself was because she had not thought of herself as beautiful or valuable.

True self-awareness will eliminate the distorted negative self-concept that leads people to be self-destructive.

The Rewards of Sobriety
❦

Rewards can be mature or juvenile.

Children have to be bribed to do things that are for their own good, because they lack the capacity to understand. They understand candy and toys, so these are used as incentives.

Adults should know better. The reward for living a healthy life is contained within itself: good health. The reward for living a spiritual life is the dignity of knowing that we have elevated ourselves beyond the biological concept of *Homo sapiens*, a baboon with intellect. The reward for being sober is sobriety.

We often hear about the child within us. Sometimes that consists of a juvenile insistence on external reward for doing anything that displeases us. Avoiding chemicals and coping with reality may not be pleasant, and the child within us may want some tangible reward for tolerating this discomfort.

But the adult that houses this juvenile should triumph. We should be satisfied with the true reward for being sober: sobriety.

Sponsors Bring a Healthy Perspective
❦

Coping with reality depends on how it is perceived.

Being totally inept at drawing a circle, and not too much better at drawing a straight line, I always marveled at artists able to draw pictures with photographic precision.

I was much surprised to read that artists do not have special manual dexterity. The reason they can draw so well is not that they have superior *hands*, but rather that they have superior *perception*. We can all draw what we see. Artists just see things more accurately.

Likewise, how we adapt to and cope with reality is not a function of our skill but of how we perceive reality. The more accurately we perceive it, the greater our success in dealing with it.

It is obvious why frequent contact with sponsors and veterans in recovery enhances our sobriety and functioning. They help us correct our misperceptions of reality.

A Guide For Life

The recovery program can have wide application.

A boyhood friend whom I had not seen for twenty-five years told me that he was a severe asthmatic. In addition to taking fourteen pills daily he had to take five treatments each day on a respiratory machine. Asthma, not chemicals, had made his life unmanageable.

His rabbi, who had become interested in the spirituality of the Twelve Step program, suggested he go to AA meetings. "I thought this was crazy," he said, "because I do not drink. But I was so desperate that I would have listened to anything."

"I attended AA meetings, and realizing that my life had become unmanageable, I decided to turn it over to a Higher Power just like an alcoholic. I have now been off the respirator for four months, and I am down to four pills a day. My doctor cannot understand this but says, 'whatever you are doing, just keep on doing it. It's working.' "

This reinforces the theme of my book *Waking Up Just in Time*, where I show that the Twelve Steps are an excellent guide to living for everyone, not just the addict. And the reason to work the program is as the doctor said, "It works!"

Don't Cheat Yourself

Half measures avail us nothing.

Have you ever baked a cake that turned out terribly because you omitted one ingredient? Some relapsers contend that they continued to attend meetings until their relapse, but admit that they failed to maintain contact with their sponsor.

The recovery program, like a recipe, will not produce the desired result unless *all* the ingredients are present. A sponsor is a vital ingredient. Sponsors tell us what we *need to hear* instead of what we *like* to hear. They alert us when we are deviating from the program.

Addiction is very cunning. It can lead us to believe that we are safe just because we are attending meetings. Meetings are vital, but we should not deceive ourselves by thinking that we are working a quality program if we are not relating regularly to our sponsors.

It Doesn't Matter Where You Are
🍎

We must always put principles above personalities.

A person with six years of sobriety moved to another city, contacted AA, and established a relationship with a new sponsor. Nevertheless, he soon relapsed.

"I attended some meetings," he said, "but it was just not the same. The place where you got your original sobriety has some kind of magic. The meetings here never felt the same."

The principles of AA and NA are the same everywhere, and the Steps are no different in Oregon than in Virginia, or in Spain or Finland. When sobriety is based on AA principles, change of location has no effect.

What is different in a new place are the people. This person had stayed sober primarily to earn the respect of his friends, because it was unthinkable to disappoint them. The new location offered him the same principles but not the same personalities.

If you are in a new location, do not let this affect you. Continue faithful adherence to the Twelve Step program, and you can be sober anywhere.

Letting Go Doesn't Mean Copping Out
❦

Dependence on a Higher Power is not an abdication of responsibility.

Some people criticize AA and NA as fostering dependence and encouraging "copping out." But if we look at people who are in recovery, we see people at their jobs daily, whether as laborers, housewives, or professionals. No one sits back and says, "I'm going to the beach today. Let God do all the work."

Turning things over to God allows us to use our abilities. Some people are unable to use their capacities because of anxiety. Panic is destructive, and people have been trampled to death when they panic.

But relying on a Higher Power prevents this paralyzing panic. We are capable of using our abilities to get things done for ourselves.

Lessons From Nature

Nature is a great teacher.

I had the opportunity to observe salmon swim up-stream to lay their eggs in the same place as where they were born. They swam against the tide and jumped up powerful cascades to reach a higher level. If they missed on the first try, they tried again.

Would the salmon go back if they did not have to fight against gravity? Who knows. Perhaps it is the fight against powerful forces that stimulates them.

Salmon have an instinctive goal. Humans have an intellectual goal. Like salmon, we are stimulated by the resistances we meet to strive ever higher, to get where we know we belong.

Another thing we can learn from the salmon is that they never jump two levels at once. Easy does it. One level at a time.

New Opportunities For Addiction
❦

Why are chemicals baffling?

A physician with ten years of quality sobriety, who was on the staff of a rehab center, developed high blood pressure, for which his doctor prescribed Valium. The physician explained that he could not use Valium because, as a recovering addict, he was prone to abuse it. The doctor suggested that his wife keep the medication and dispense one tablet four times daily.

"When my wife gave me the first pill, I put it in my pocket, and saved up all four pills so that I could get a buzz taking them together." Within several days he had relapsed into full-blown addiction.

That an intelligent person who is actively involved in treating addiction and understands it thoroughly can do something so self-destructive is nothing less than baffling.

We are always recover*ing*. We must always be on guard, because chemicals are baffling.

Sobriety Can Bring New Problems
🍎

Abstinence does not eliminate all problems.

A man set up a workshop in his apartment. Because the noise of the drilling and other machinery was so annoying, a neighbor began playing loud music to obscure the noise. When the man later moved his workshop elsewhere, he became annoyed by the neighbor's loud music. But by this time the neighbor had come to enjoy it, and did not wish to stop it.

In a similar vein, the sober spouse may have to adapt to the addict's behavior. These adaptations then become an established pattern that may be difficult to change when the addict stops chemical use. The addict is now annoyed with the things the spouse does, which had come about as a response to the addiction.

This is why codependency requires careful attention. Abstinence can create a new set of problems.

Appreciate The Good Things You Have
🌹

Sometimes we need lessons in gratitude.

One day I had allowed myself to become upset because the cruise control on my new car was not functioning. It was hardly something to cause a foul mood, but I let it do exactly that.

That day a young woman who was in early recovery reported how thrilled she was that things were going better for her now that she was sober. She had found an apartment she could afford and a full-time job, albeit at minimum wage. Soon she might have enough money to repair her car, which did not run in reverse.

"How can you drive without reverse?" I asked.

"It takes a little calculation and a lot of prayer," she answered. "But I must remember that some people don't even have a car."

I became much more appreciative of my new car, which had everything except cruise control. We should learn how to appreciate the things we have.

Unburden Yourself of Things You Cannot Control

❦

What do we do when there is nothing we can do?

Late one night I received a call to my unlisted number. The operator asked if I would accept the call, and I accepted even though I did not know the caller—perhaps it was an emergency. When the caller asked for psychiatric advice, I responded in anger that it was an audacity to call me collect for this. Although the caller protested that she had not called collect, I hung up the phone.

I later reflected that perhaps the operator had asked for me person-to-person rather than to accept the charges. If so, I had unjustly accused the woman. I could not apologize to her because I did not know who she was.

The anger at myself persisted until I had an opportunity to share this at a meeting. I realized that since I could not make amends, I must turn this incident over to God. All I could do was to be more patient before making judgments. I was able to get relief because, having turned it over, the burden was no longer on me.

"Easy Does It" Can Require Hard Work

❦

"Easy does it" does not mean that we should look for the easiest way to get something done.

Some people with eating disorders have undergone intestinal bypass surgery to lose weight. But though initially successful, they may regain weight after several years. A change in life-style such as with the Overeaters Anonymous program is not as easy a method, but it can give more lasting results.

I was asked about the possibility of learning by listening to a tape while asleep. I don't know whether this works, but on principle, trying to gain knowledge without the effort of studying isn't profitable.

"Easy does it" means that we do not let ourselves get into a dither about things. Getting something accomplished, however, requires elbow grease.

There Are A Million Excuses
❧

Keep coming back. It works.

Do you need an excuse for not attending meetings? Don't rack your brain. Just write to me, and I will send you as many as you need. These are excellent excuses, collected from people who have relapsed.

Some excuses are amateurish, such as "I saw one guy leave a meeting and go directly to a bar." This is silly, since it doesn't mention that the other eighty-nine people who were at the meeting went home and stayed sober.

There are much better excuses, such as the therapist who said, "I've been sober for thirteen years. I work with addicts all day, and I don't need another hour of associating with addicts at night." This is perfectly logical and reasonable, but nevertheless the therapist got drunk.

If you continue with meetings, you are likely to remain sober. If you discontinue meetings, there is a high risk of relapse, regardless of how good your excuses are.

Life Is Always a Struggle
🍂

Living a moral life can never be completely tranquil.

Books on peace of mind or peace of soul can mislead us into thinking that complete inner peace is achievable.

Life is full of stress and tension. In addition to external stress, there is an internal ongoing struggle. We have many biological drives. Many of our impulses are in direct contradiction to our beliefs. The ongoing battle between these two forces rarely subsides. Our impulses want gratification, and our conscience says no.

Although complete inner peace is thus never possible, the idea that it is feasible can lead us to try and achieve it via chemicals. The brief period of chemical tranquillity comes at an exorbitant price.

We should understand that absolute tranquillity is not achievable, and that realistic peace of mind exists with some coexisting stress and tension.

Sharing Versus Using
❧

There is using, and there is using.

A gentleman told me once how he *used* people during his addiction, manipulating everyone for his own needs. When he called his mother during early recovery and she asked, "What do you want?" he told her that he was just calling to find out how she was feeling. She was in disbelief, because during his addiction he never called unless he wanted money or an attorney.

In sobriety, this gentleman now *uses* people instead of chemicals. However, this use is constructive. He uses services and compensates for them, or shares with others as they share with him, or accepts a sincere helping hand when reality is too much to handle. This is totally different from the way he exploited people during active addiction, without appreciation or gratitude.

No person is an island, and no one can ever be totally independent. The dependence of the Twelve Step program is a mutual relationship rather than one of exploitation.

Experiencing Forgiveness
❦

Words have meaning only if we have the experience.

The idea of a fourth dimension is meaningless. Even ideas such as eternity, or infinity can set our mind spinning if we think about them deeply. We have never encountered anything that did not have a beginning. A child will ask, "Where did God come from," but adults who know that there is no answer to this simply don't ask the question.

We are told that we should feel relieved of guilt if we repent something and ask for forgiveness. Some people are unable to break loose from guilt. Perhaps this is because *forgiveness* is just a word, totally foreign to their own experience.

If you find yourself overwhelmed with guilt even after you have made amends and asked for forgiveness, there may be something more you must do. You must sincerely forgive someone who has offended or harmed you. Once you have experienced forgiveness by forgiving someone else, you'll understand the meaning of the word, and realize that you, too, can be forgiven.

The Futile Pursuit of Perfection

We must accept our fallibility.

A young student nurse cried uncontrollably because she had made a harmless medication error: "I'm going to quit nursing school. If I can make an error in medication, I may someday kill someone. I don't belong in nursing."

If every nurse who felt that way quit, we would have only nurses who don't care if they made a mistake.

I am vulnerable to being sick and needing medical care. Who is going to be my nurse? Someone who is perfect and never makes a mistake? I don't believe that there are such people. I don't want my life in the hands of a nurse who never gets upset about a mistake.

Sometimes we are hard on ourselves because of our mistakes. That keeps us on the alert, taking precautions to avoid further mistakes. It also leads us to make amends. But after we are finished being harsh with ourselves, we should accept our humanity and our fallibility. We need to try to do the very best we can, with the knowledge that we cannot possibly be perfect.

Is Recovery a Rebirth?

❦

Not every recovery is a rebirth—but some are.

Some people who recover from addiction realize that, although their first chemical use occurred in adolescence, they have had a distorted view of themselves and of the world for as long as they can recall. Even as young children, they felt themselves to be defective and the world around them to be hostile and unfair. In recovery we begin to recognize these misperceptions or misconceptions. As distortions of reality, they technically are manifestations of insanity. How then can we ask to be "restored" to a sanity we never had?

For some people, it may be necessary to go all the way back to the moment of birth. (It is unlikely that we had any ideas of our self and the world during intrauterine life.) At first breath, the infant has sanity. Perhaps a delay in providing a bottle or changing a wet diaper left the impression that the world is an unkind place. Our ideas of reality begin to form in the first few days of life, but at birth we are all "sane."

Recovery then is a rebirth, and we can be "restored" to that pristine sanity.

The Joy of Giving
❦

Helping others is self-help.

Pain is all-encompassing. If we have a severe toothache we think of nothing else. This is equally true of emotional pain. If we are deeply depressed, there is nothing that can divert our attention.

We have seen people struggling to overcome the impulse to drink or use chemicals, depressed by a disruption of the family, loss of job, or trouble with the law—all incident to their addiction. Yet when faced with someone who is in addictive trouble, they are open, empathic, receptive, and willing to help. When suffering people are so willing to help others, they are distracted from their own distress.

This is the magic of the Twelve Step program. It enables us to look outside of ourselves. If more people would reach out and help someone instead of retreating into self-pity when they are in the throes of misery, the world would be a much more pleasant place to live.

Restraint is Often the Best Response
❦

Patience can help avoid distress.

I once pulled into a parking lot, and being fifth in a procession, was annoyed that the lead car was moving at a snail's pace. The driver in front of me tooted angrily. Although tempted to pound on the horn, I decided not to add to the noise. When the lead car pulled into a parking space, I saw the handicap symbol on its license plate. I felt badly that I had harbored angry feelings at a handicapped person who was searching for the nearest place to park. I was grateful that I had restrained myself from sounding the horn.

While we may make amends for having offended someone, it would be so much better if we could avoid the incident in the first place. This is possible if we delay our reaction, rather than behave in a knee-jerk fashion.

What a peaceful night's sleep we would have if we could retire with the thought "There is not one thing I did today that I regret having done." For many people, this would eliminate the need for sedatives.

The Difference Between Knowledge and Wisdom

Knowledge is not enough.

A competent therapist discovered that his daughter was using cocaine. He reacted like any other parent, with the usual combination of denial, rationalization, projection, anger, and attempt to control, although he would have counseled other parents to act differently. The reason? He counseled other parents with his *knowledge*, but he reacted to his own child with his *emotions*.

Knowledge resides in the conscious part of our mind and emotion in the unconscious. The two do not always function in harmony.

Emotions are powerful. They may also be misleading, regardless of how knowledgeable we are. Thus, we may not act constructively. It is as unwise to be your own addiction counselor as to be your own doctor or lawyer. That is why we need outside expertise to guide us, whether it is in regard to ourselves or to someone we love.

Greatness Comes with Humility

Gratitude results in humility.

A person who receives a Divine favor may consider himself superior to others, and become arrogant instead of humble. Rarely is such a person grateful to God. Indeed, he may think God as fortunate in having so wonderful a subject!

If we recognize Divine providence and realize that we are the beneficiaries of God's kindnesses, we become closer to Him. Standing in the eminent presence of the Infinite makes us feel very small indeed. This humility and self-effacement is in no way demeaning. To the contrary, the privilege of being a subject to the Great Sovereign is edifying.

The measure of a person's greatness is in his ability to be grateful and humble.

Mental Vigilance
❧

If something is really important, it never leaves our mind.

Nursing mothers are the world's soundest sleepers and will not be woken by the loudest thunder. Yet just a whimper from the infant will promptly arouse them. This is because mothers are conditioned to respond to their baby's needs. Whether in a deep sleep or occupied in some activity, mothers remain in emotional contact with their baby.

The person to whom sobriety is of preeminent importance may be occupied in some activity, not thinking about sobriety. However, should anything occur to threaten that sobriety, there is an immediate arousal and a recall of all that is necessary to protect the sobriety.

Devotion to AA and NA principles need not divert us from our normal functions any more than a mother's devotion to her infant prevents her from engaging in other activities.

Know When to Relax

It has been said that the most important time to relax is when we have no time to relax. But what can we do if we are so busy that we cannot take the time to relax?

Just consider priorities. A tourist who was told that there were no vacancies at a motel said to the manager, "If the president came here tonight you would find a room for him, wouldn't you?"

"Well, of course," the manager said.

"Good! The president isn't coming, so you can give me that room."

If we had a heart attack, we would have the time to rest. So let us use the time that we would have used for recuperation for healthy relaxation instead.

If we make relaxation a priority, we will find the time for it.

Don't Place Yourself in Harm's Way
❦

There is good reason to change "people, places, and things."

We consider addiction a disease. Further, we dispute people who consider it a self-inflicted disease. Indeed, there is evidence that addiction is strongly influenced by genetics and biology, and not self-inflicted.

Yet we cannot absolve ourselves of all responsibility. The person who is blown off the roof by a powerful wind must have been standing near the edge, in a hazardous position.

The people, places, and things that were associated with our alcohol or drug use are hazardous to our sobriety, and we should not expose ourselves to these dangers. Similarly, we cannot claim that our improper behavior was due to circumstances if we knowingly placed ourselves in those circumstances.

It Takes More Than Just Drugs to Make an Addict

❦

The real difference between chemically dependent and nondependent people is that the former use chemicals and the latter do not.

This is not being facetious. The question is often asked whether there is a personality profile for an addict. Could a thorough psychological evaluation predict who will become an addict? The answer is that there is nothing in the psychological makeup of the preaddict that distinguishes him or her from the nonaddict.

When addicts discontinue their use of chemicals, they are nevertheless vulnerable to the same errors in adjusting to life as during addiction. This is why continued involvement in the recovery program is essential. Complacency and failure to work the program can allow a recurrence of the same errors of omission or commission in sobriety that we had during active addiction.

Unreasonable Desires Can Be Deadly

Endless pursuits can be lethal.

Seeking sobriety from chemicals can indeed help us find serenity. Addiction to chemicals has shown us that some of our desires can be insatiable. The quantity of chemicals we needed constantly increased, until "enough" constituted a lethal dose. But as we recover, we apply this knowledge to other desires, whether for food, money, sex, or acclaim.

There is the fable of a greedy person who found a magic purse. Whenever he took out a dollar, another dollar appeared in its place. Several days later he was found dead among a huge pile of dollars. His greed obscured his need for food or water and he died of starvation, driven by his desire to get just one more dollar.

Recovery from addiction has taught us that some desires can be deadly.

Fellowship Can Remove Many Barriers

🍃

Fellowship enhances serenity.

Many people pursue individual goals, often pushing others out of the way. When they reach their goal, they discover that they are alone. They must enjoy their achievement in absolute solitude because they have alienated others along the way.

Many chemically addicted people are loners. They associate with others only when obtunded by chemicals. But recovery enables us to escape from the confinements we have built to protect us from others. These walls became a prison in which we trapped ourselves.

The recovery fellowship allows us to share with others—to help and to be helped—and we thereby escape from our prison to serenity.

Understanding Destructive Behavior
❦

Exercise care in interpreting others' behavior.

An adolescent whose antics caused his parents a great deal of aggravation was given psychological tests, one of which included sentence completions. He completed a sentence that began "I wish . . ." with the words "that my parents knew how much I love them."

This young man's behavior hardly indicated love for his parents. However, recovering addicts can understand this because they know the pain of having hurt those whom they loved.

Destructive behavior cannot be tolerated, regardless of the motivation. We may have to take firm measures in relating to people who behave this way. We should bear in mind, though, that just as tough love is well intended, behavior that is defiant may emanate from someone who nevertheless loves us.

Denying the Obvious

Addictive thinking includes strange denials.

A compulsive gambler who had been economically ruined by gambling twice previously this time lost his family as well as his fortune. Yet he was adamant in his ability to win, stating, "I have a system that is guaranteed to beat the horses." His therapist asked, "How can you say that? This is the third time you have been wiped out and are in total ruin."

The gambler answered, "I have a winning system, but when I get to the track I get so excited that I don't put my system into operation. When I put the system into function, I know I will win."

Can you think of anything so insane as a person in total ruin still believing that he is a winner? And planning to continue the same activities that brought on his disaster?

Whether it is gambling, chemicals, food, or sex, the story is always the same: the addict has an ingenious way of denying the obvious.

Adjust to Reality

Someone said once that we want facts to fit our preconceptions. When they don't, it is easier to ignore the facts than to change the preconceptions.

An optimum adjustment to reality can be made only if we perceive reality correctly. A distorted perception of reality invariably leads to maladjustment.

Reality consists of hard facts, which exist whether we like them or not. Ignoring facts, for whatever reason, is going to result in problems.

We might not like the fact that the economy is in a recession, our job is in jeopardy, our son or daughter is marrying the wrong person, or someone we love has a chemical problem. However, ignoring these facts will only make a bad situation worse.

Ignoring facts is just another word for denial, the hallmark of addiction. When facts and preconceptions conflict, the latter must be modified.

Hard Work and Simple Solutions
🐛

Simple solutions are not always correct.

There is a cartoon that shows a child sitting on Santa Claus's knee. The child asks, "Why can't you just legalize being naughty?" This is the way some young people may think. They feel everything should be legalized: marijuana, heroin, cocaine.

While Prohibition was a failure, it is also evident that legalizing alcohol has not eliminated the disastrous consequences of alcoholism. What are needed in our culture are more self-restraint and self-discipline. Unfortunately, while the voices for legalizing drugs are loud, advocates of self-restraint are few and far between. Self-restraint is not a popular message.

Recovering people have learned the hard way that only discipline prevents self-destruction. It would be well if society appreciated this and made a greater effort to avoid simple solutions.

Are You Missing Something?

I have often heard people say, "I never drink to get high, only to feel normal."

What is normal? We make assumptions about what is normal based on our observations of other people. We see people smiling, apparently working satisfactorily at their jobs. They seem to have a pleasant relationship with their spouse or partner. If we don't feel like smiling—or are frustrated with our job, or are not getting along well with our spouse or partner—we feel cheated. "Why don't I have what other people have?" we ask.

A recovering person said, "I always compared my *insides* to other people's *outsides*." People may indeed be smiling although they do not feel like smiling; they may not be showing their dissatisfaction with their job; and their domestic relationshp may not be as it seems in public.

Most people feel no more and no less satisfaction or frustration than you do. If you are not aware of this it is because you are comparing your "insides" with other people's "outsides."

How Can We Remain Indifferent?

Hatred is a despicable emotion. Indifference is even worse.

If we argue with someone and she does not respond, we find it more annoying than if she would overtly disagree with us. Why? Because even a hostile response acknowledges our existence, whereas ignoring a person is essentially saying, "You don't count at all."

People crave acknowledgment. Remember the class clown who was repeatedly evicted from the classroom? He was willing to accept rebuke and ridicule because of his desperate need to call attention to himself.

We may not realize that people have been offended when we fail to notice them. It takes so little effort to make people feel good. A pleasant greeting, an offer of a cup of coffee, an inquiry whether they might need a ride home.

Probably we have all experienced the displeasure of being ignored. Let us avoid doing this to others. Little things can mean so much.

Stooping to New Lows

We behave according to our self-worth.

In a discussion of the U.S. economy, it was mentioned that the dollar had fallen to an all-time low. Someone commented that, regardless of how low the dollar fell, it would never fall so low that people won't stoop to pick it up.

If you drop a coin in the mud, and you are wearing a fine garment, you are unlikely to risk getting soiled in order to retrieve the coin. You recognize that you cannot get into the mud without getting dirty.

Yet when it comes to decency, people may stoop very low to earn a dollar. Either they do not recognize that stooping to unethical behavior will soil their character, or they think so little of themselves that they do not see anything wrong with getting dirty.

We do things during active addiction that are beneath our dignity, probably because we do not feel dignified. As we recover, our increased sense of self-worth not only prevents our relapse into chemical use but also disallows all indecent and unethical behavior.

Out of Control

Control is an important issue in addiction.

The incidence of chemical dependency, especially among young people, is probably greater today than in the past.

When travel was primarily by horse and buggy, the driver did not actually control the horse, but by pulling on the reins he coerced the horse to choose to turn. Today's driver does not make the car choose, but he actually *controls* its direction.

Little children enjoy toys with remote controls. Scientists at the space center control the movements of a satellite a billion miles away.

Technology has provided us with unprecedented controls. We have come to believe in our ability to control everything. This contributes to the delusion that we can also control chemicals.

We should not let technology delude us. We cannot control our use of chemicals.

The Difference Between Need and Desire

🍂

What are our real needs?

The philosopher Immanuel Kant, upon seeing a display of items in a shop window, said, "I never knew there are so many things I can get along without."

Most people are preoccupied with their needs. It would be to our advantage if we thought more about how many of these things we do *not* need. If we look at our belongings, we are likely to find things we rarely use, yet when we bought them we were certain we needed them. The idea "I need" is one that often escapes our critical judgment.

We often want many things we do not really need. An alcoholic once said, "I never drank unless I thought it was exactly what I needed to do at just that moment." There is a difference between "I want," and "I need."

The recovery program teaches us to say, "I really don't need this chemical today. Whether I will need it tomorrow, I can decide tomorrow."

When we turn our lives over to the will of a Higher Power, we can eliminate those things we want that are destructive, and concentrate on our constructive *needs*.

An "All or Nothing" Struggle

Only 100 percent will work.

Chemicals are indeed enemies, and they are cunning. In addiction, chemicals may look for any possible entry. The addiction may cause insomnia, pain, or anxiety— all in order to get us to take an addictive chemical. Our only defense against relapse is to block *all* portals of entry. Any opening, any side door, any weakness in the wall, can provide a means of entry.

The statement "half measures avail us nothing" may be taken to mean that three-quarter measures *will* work. The fact is that anything less than 100 percent is fraught with risk. The 1 percent unguarded point is a point of entry.

This is why we must remain in contact with the program indefinitely and practice its principles in *all* our affairs. The one time we do not practice the principles of recovery is our Achilles' heel of relapse.

Excuses Get Us Nowhere

"No one has ever excused his way to success."

Perhaps it is a carryover from the notes we brought our grade-school teachers to explain our absences, but many people believe that excuses have value in life. But as any authority on how to succeed has pointed out, no one has ever achieved success via the avenue of excuses.

Recovering people do not need to be taught this. If a Nobel Prize were given for excellence in rationalization, addicts would win hands down. No one can concoct as many excuses as an addict.

These champions can also testify to the futility of even the most ingenious excuse. Good performance and responsible behavior are what succeed. Poor performance and irresponsibility always fail.

Recovering people know this, but a reminder never hurts.

Be Wise Enough to Ask for Help
❦

A Danish proverb: Better to ask twice than to lose your way once.

With some automobile drivers, it is a matter of pride. They will not stop to ask directions, insisting they know the way. Only after they are undeniably lost do they swallow their pride and discover they had been driving in the wrong direction.

It is annoying when a failure to ask for guidance wastes time and gasoline. But it is more serious when we have gone the wrong direction in life, and some of our mistakes are irreversible.

Career and marriage are important decisions, but they are not the only major decisions in life. Everyone can benefit from guidance. Recovering addicts are convincing instructors of the importance of asking for guidance, rather than assuming that we know it all.

Wisdom is not in knowing everything but in knowing when to ask.

Recovering Our Emotions
🍏

Communication is the ability to also hear what is *not* being said.

Our minds comprise two parts: intellect and emotions. We communicate to and from the intellect with words, but emotional messages are communicated nonverbally through eye contact, gestures, and tone inflection.

Chemicals affect the emotions first, so it is possible to continue communicating intellectually even after the emotional transmitter and receiver have been disabled. During active addiction it is possible to function intellectually—give lectures, perform operations, try cases, audit books—though all emotional contact has ceased.

When we recover, we restore the emotional system and can resume full communication. We might not always be pleased with those emotional communications, and that is why there is always a risk of relapse. But as recovery progresses, we learn how to deal with emotions, and we can then enjoy total communication.

Life-or-Death Struggles
🍂

When everything is a life-or-death matter, we die many times.

Some people think only in extremes; solutions to problems must be either one or the other. There is no compromise or negotiation. This thinking results in unnecessary radical measures, with dissatisfaction to all concerned.

This is a frequent trait among addicts, and contributes to chemical use. Some people resort to chemicals as an escape when they see no solution to their problems. But problems can always be resolved, albeit not in the manner one might wish.

In this sense, addiction generates a vicious cycle. When chemicals are used to escape from problems that could be resolved by compromise, our perception and judgment become impaired, so that each problem takes on greater significance and appears even more insoluble. When everything becomes a life-or-death matter, we die many times.

"Easy does it" means sitting back and reevaluating problems for possible solutions. Sobriety helps us achieve this.

Be Receptive to Wisdom
🍎

The AA Grapevine stated, "Fear is a darkroom where negatives are developed."

This metaphor means that, under the influence of fear, we are in the dark and lose our perception, resulting in negative thoughts and feelings.

But metaphors are malleable, and we can bend them every which way. For instance, darkrooms are where productive work gets done. Negatives are converted to positives by placing the negative over sensitive photographic paper and exposing it briefly to light until a clear picture emerges. Even momentary exposure to light can convert the negative to a positive.

Let us do this in our own lives. Find a source of illumination: *wisdom* from a reliable source. Be receptive and sensitive. Expose yourself to the source of illumination. There is a high probability that a positive picture will result. And although the negative image was useless, the positive image can be helpful.

In the recovery program, it is said that if life gives you lemons, make lemonade. This restates the concept of converting the negative into the positive—which is what recovery is all about.

Freedom Brings Responsibility
❦

The psychological problems that complicate addiction began long before use of chemicals.

It has been said that it is easy to take liberty for granted when you have never had it taken from you. Inasmuch as we lose freedom and become a slave to addiction, why don't addicts feel deprived of the precious freedom they once had?

The answer is that many addicts never experienced freedom even before they began using chemicals. They may have been subject to compulsions, to rigid habits, to an inability to say no, to being dominated by others, or to any life-style that did not allow freedom of thought and action. When chemicals came along, they just took their place alongside the other problems.

For many addicts, recovery is the first taste of liberty. As wonderful as this is, it carries the responsibility of making decisions, of weighing options, and of considering many factors before choosing what to do. Of course freedom is better, but it is not always easy, and we must always beware the tendency to fall back on what is easier, even when it is to our detriment.

Attitude Adjustments

The philosopher William James said, "The greatest discovery of my generation is that a human being can alter his life by altering his attitude."

Many people think that changing their life requires major upheavals, such as relocating, changing jobs, getting married or divorced. Not so. The circumstances can remain exactly as they are. A radical change in our life can come about simply by changing our attitude.

A recovering person once said, "I discovered my attitude was that my family was to give me everything my parents did. When my wife did not do somersaults over every little accomplishment of mine, I was offended. When she did not dote on me when I was sick the way my parents did, I became irate. I was being mistreated. When my attitude changed and I realized she was my wife and not my mother, I stopped my bizarre behavior."

We often bring inappropriate attitudes to addiction. If we change these when we become sober, our lives become much more livable.

Make Peace With Yourself

We are important to ourselves.

A recovering person showed his sponsor a list of everyone to whom he would make amends, and was told the list was incomplete. He was perplexed. How could the sponsor know whom he had offended?

"You forgot to put yourself at the top of the list," the sponsor said.

Even if we were totally isolated, and had never harmed anyone else, chemical use certainly harms ourselves. All the amends in the world are inadequate for full recovery unless we realize that we have no right whatever to damage ourselves.

Coming into recovery, we may not feel very good about ourselves. The most brilliant and dazzling diamond does not look beautiful when it is first drawn from the mine. It needs to be polished so that its beauty and value can be perceived and appreciated by all. That must happen in recovery.

We must make amends to ourselves for having injured something so valuable as ourselves.

It's Not Always Easy to Take Advice
❦

Profiting from good advice requires more wisdom than giving advice.

It is fascinating to observe others in the recovery program. People with the least experience are fountains of advice, whereas seasoned veterans often sit quietly. Although they gladly respond to questions, they do not volunteer advice. For those seeking guidance, therefore, look among those who are maintaining their silence.

Accepting good advice is not easy. Very often we must make some major modifications in our life-style to achieve sobriety. But if what we are instructed to do is not inconvenient, we should suspect its authenticity.

Veterans in the recovery program say, "Just listen and do as you're told." No one likes to hear this, but it is good advice. The behavior of active addiction was largely doing what we wanted to do, rather than what we should do. Recovery requires a reversal of this.

Don't Be Afraid of Real Sorrow
🍃

Recovery concepts are sometimes grossly distorted.

A woman with years of sobriety related the difficulties she experienced during her husband's illness and following his death. She stated, "I put on the best front I can at work. I guess I'm not working the program well."

She felt she was derelict because she was feeling sorry for herself. Some people in the program told her that she must learn how to be happy all the time.

This is a distortion of the program's teachings. AA and NA are programs of reality, and grieving for the loss of a loved one is reality. The program does not disapprove of normal emotions.

But when a person experiences setbacks because of chemical use, such as the breakup of a marriage or the loss of a job, and says, "Poor me! Why do these things happen to me?" that is what is meant by a "pity party." The program is critical of feeling sorry for yourself and blaming everyone else for the consequences of your addictive behavior. However, when you feel genuine grief from loss of a loved one, that is a healthy emotion.

We must be careful not to distort the wonderful ideas of the program. When in doubt, check with senior people in sobriety who can tell you what these concepts really mean.

Fear Can Destroy You
🍎

Fear is not only an *effect* of distress but may also *cause* distress.

If we were asked to walk on a plank set on the floor, we would have little difficulty doing so. If that same plank were suspended high in the air, the fear of falling might be so great and cause such anxiety that we could not keep our balance. The fear would actually cause us to fall.

This phenomenon is true of chemical relapse as well. We may be so terrified of relapse, and work ourselves into so intense a state of panic, that we are driven to take a chemical for relief.

This can also occur with any task where we fear failure. Many bright students have failed exams because their minds went blank owing to the fear of not doing well.

Easy does it. Putting things in their proper perspective, taking a challenge one bit at a time, and trusting in our Higher Power can help us avoid the destructive panic.

Make the Wise Choice

When we turn our will over to a Higher Power we do not lose the ability to choose.

If a child receives a gift of money, she could spend it all at the candy or toy store, and have nothing to show other than a stomachache or a broken toy. Or a wise child can give the money to a parent to invest. This second option does not mean surrender of choice. She made a wise choice by turning the money over to a parent who knew better what to do with it.

When we turn our will over to a Higher Power, we do not surrender our ability to choose. Rather, by realizing that our will can get us into trouble, we make a free choice to adopt the will of a Higher Power as a guide through life.

Chemicals are not the only foolish choice a person can make. Desires and temptations can lead to many things that are to our detriment. We can avoid being blinded by temptation if we adopt the will of a Higher Power.

Are You Killing Time?

Time is a valuable and irreplaceable commodity.

While our culture is preoccupied with saving time—microwave ovens, fax machines, jet flight, high-speed copiers—it also extravagantly wastes time. It is not unusual to hear a person say, "I've got some time to kill," and then spend hours doing something meaningless. It is strange that seconds and minutes can be so valuable, yet hours can be worthless.

Some people have turned to chemicals because of boredom. Addiction sometimes has its onset in retirees who do not know what to do with the time that had previously been occupied by work.

Whether working or not, we should set goals in our lives that enable us to put time to good use. The time saved by our advanced technology should be a blessing, not a curse.

Changing Ourselves to Face Reality
❦

The backbone of recovery is the Serenity Prayer.

> God grant me the serenity to accept that which
> I cannot change, the courage to change that
> which I can, and the wisdom to know the dif-
> ference.

One person had this version of the Serenity Prayer:
God grant me the courage to change those people I
cannot accept.

What we may *not* be able to change is the rest of the
world. Our best chance for change is in ourselves. Isn't
it strange, though, that so many people accept *themselves* as fixed entities and expect the rest of the world
to change to accommodate *them*? People who achieve
true sobriety know that this way of thinking leads only
to disappointment and frustration.

When reality doesn't change to suit us, some people
drink or take drugs. All this does is makes us imagine,
at least temporarily, that reality has changed. Living in
a make-believe world is a kind of insanity.

Reality is often very difficult. At times, it can be enjoyable, frequently it is just barely tolerable, but it is never
totally impossible. Being sober means adjusting to reality. And this adjustment is usually accomplished by making the necessary changes in *ourselves*, not in others.

Recognize What is Worth Worrying About

An axiom of recovery is "One day at a time."

This does *not* mean that we just live for today and don't give a thought to the future. That's a far cry from sober thought, and is the kind of irresponsible thinking that leads to chemical use.

Responsible planning for the future is part of sobriety. "One day at a time" means that we don't take on anything today that we can't do anything about today. We don't waste valuable time worrying about something that is out of our hands.

Assume you have an important exam coming up that you must pass to get a license. Before you take the exam, worrying is constructive because you can study instead of whiling away your time. However, after the exam, when you must wait for the results, worrying is destructive. All the worrying in the world will not affect the result.

You may think, "What do I do if I fail the exam?" That's where we say, "One day at a time." You will have time to cross that bridge if you have to. If you spend time in "constructive worrying"—that is, in preparation before the exam—there will be little need to worry afterward.

Do what you can today, but if something is out of your hands, turn it over to a Higher Power. You'll be less exhausted, as well as happier and sober.

Don't Let Your Guard Down to Addiction

❧

Our enemy is alcohol and drugs.

If I were your mortal enemy, I would not attack you when you were expecting it and were on guard. I would keep out of sight for a while, so that you would not think about me. Then I would pass by and wave, "Hello there, Bill," and go on my way. This would make you think, "I thought that guy hated my guts, but he sure looked friendly enough!" I would repeat this until you began thinking, "I must have figured him all wrong. He sure seems to be a pleasant fellow."

The next time we meet I would say, "Why don't you come with me for a cup of coffee?" And I would repeat this, making every effort to be nice to you, while I cunningly plan your destruction. Eventually you would become convinced that I am a trusted friend. This gives me the opportunity. Since you will be totally off guard, I can kill you with minimum risk and effort.

This is precisely the way the chemical enemy operates. After you stop drinking or using, the chemicals may not enter your mind for months. You may then be lured into a bar "just to talk with the fellows." Eventually you think "just one beer won't hurt."

The enemy has you off your guard because he has made you think he is not only harmless but your best friend. If you don't believe this is true, just ask some people in recovery.

Get Rid of Your Resentments
❦

Rewards are slow in coming.

Jim is a brilliant corporate attorney who continued to function in spite of heavy drinking. After he became sober there was a corporate shake-up, and he found himself out of a job. Not having saved anything during his drinking, he was broke.

Jim was contacted by a group of investors to organize a chain of specialty stores. After the first several became operative, he was voted out, and it was obvious he had been exploited.

Jim struggled to support his family, and stated that he was very resentful of the group that had exploited him. "But I will go to an AA meeting tonight," he said, "and drop off my resentments. If I don't get rid of my resentments, I will drink again."

Jim and others like him are fortunate. They know that resentments are dangerous. What about all those people who are not chemically dependent? They do not have a program that teaches the danger of harboring resentments, which may cause peptic ulcers, high blood pressure, migraines, and other physical or emotional disorders.

Jim ultimately was rewarded with a good job and an even higher salary. His greatest reward, however, is the personality growth he achieved in sobriety—something difficult to acquire any other way.

Don't Live a Masquerade

Acting "as if" may or may not be good.

Some behaviors are constructive, but if we have not been accustomed to them we may resist them. For example, we are often reluctant at first to express gratitude, say "I'm sorry," or pray. So even if we do not feel sincere in these behaviors, it is okay to act "as if." Once we overcome the resistance through practice, the real feeling will follow.

It is not good, however, to act "as if" when the behavior is deceptive—such as masquerading as something other than we are or misleading people to think you are their friend when you really despise them.

There are two things wrong with this second kind of "as if." First, you may eventually begin to believe your own lie; and second, eventually it becomes necessary to discontinue the masquerade. Ending the masquerade can be difficult. As someone said, "If the mask sticks to your face, some of your skin comes off when you remove it."

"To thine own self be true."

Learning to Cope

❧

The key to sobriety is coping.

There really are only two ways of reacting to any challenge in life: coping or escaping. There is no third option.

When a challenge is truly overwhelming, as when your car is stalled on a railroad track and a diesel engine is heading toward you, it is appropriate to escape. However, some people escape challenges that are not in fact overwhelming, but which they *think* are overwhelming. Very often their escape is to alcohol or drugs.

Challenges that are well within our capacity to cope may appear to be overwhelming if we underestimate our own strength and capability—something many of us have been doing since we were children. This is why building self-esteem is so necessary in recovery.

The underestimation that plagues many people is due to a misperception of themselves. But the self-awareness that results from diligently working the Twelve Steps can help people discover character strengths they were unaware of, as well as eliminate defects of character.

Sobriety can thus enhance our self-esteem and help us cope more effectively. Our self-esteem is then further strengthened as we do indeed cope effectively with life's challenges.

Reaching Rational Conclusions

Turning things over to a Higher Power is not as difficult as some people think.

"Let go and let God" does not mean we should move to the passenger seat and expect God to drive. We are expected to act in order to bring about the results we desire.

There are times, however, when we may have done everything we can do to reach a certain goal, and there is just nothing more we can do. In such situations, trying to do more may be counterproductive. Simple logic tells us that, at a time like this, we have to let go. Once we have done what we can, we leave the rest to God.

No one is suggesting we neglect our responsibilities and throw all the work on God. But we don't do anything when there isn't anything more constructive that we can possibly do. Before we were sober, we did not realize that there are some things we could do nothing about. We insisted on doing *everything* ourselves. This usually meant everything got all fouled up.

If you find "Let go and let God" difficult, ask yourself one simple question: "What other option is there?"

Think of it this way: turning things over and letting go and letting God is simple common sense. Sobriety is the ability to think rationally.

Admit Your Mistakes and Go On

❦

The Tenth Step of the AA program requires an ongoing personal inventory, and prompt admission of any wrong.

There is a tendency to become defensive when someone points out that we did something wrong. We often insist what we did was right. The human mind is expert at manufacturing rationalizations, or logical-sounding reasons that are just not true. These work for a time, but eventually their false nature is exposed, and we must eventually admit that what we did was indeed wrong. Not only is the failed cover-up embarrassing, but we may sometimes begin to believe our own lies—which leads to an impaired sense of judgment.

The AA program teaches "Never defend a mistake" because, the sooner you admit one, the better off and happier you will be.

Admitting a mistake may be threatening to a fragile ego, but as our sense of self-esteem increases with sobriety, the realization that we are fallible and vulnerable to do wrong is no longer devastating. Furthermore, when we promptly admit that we were wrong, we feel better for having been honest, and our self-esteem continues to grow.

You Are Not the Higher Power
❦

Some people reject AA because of its emphasis on God. They claim they do not believe in God. But difficulty with the acceptance of a Higher Power generally is an indication that we think of ourselves as the highest power.

A person whose repetitive drinking has ruined every aspect of her life, who has many times been in deep remorse but who has never been able to fulfill her sincere promises never to drink again, yet rejects help and insists that she can do it on her own, is considering herself omnipotent, and refusing to accept powerlessness. I tell such a person, only half in jest, "It is not true that you do not believe in God. You do believe in God, but you think you are Him."

I suggest to people in recovery who have difficulty with the concept of God that they take the First of the Twelve steps and admit their powerlessness. Experience has demonstrated that when we admit powerlessness over chemicals, we yield the omnipotent delusion. And when we no longer consider ourselves to be God, the difficulty in accepting a Higher Power disappears.

Knowledge or Self-Consciousness?
🍎

A true self-awareness may prevent addiction.

Some recovering alcoholics say, "I never drank to feel high. I drank just to feel normal."

Some of us are very self-conscious. When our throat or eyes are healthy, we are not aware that we have a throat or eyes. It is only when parts of our body hurt that we think of them. This is also true of the self. When our self is okay, we don't think about it. Self-consciousness is a symptom: something is wrong.

There is one important difference between physical and emotional discomfort. When a part of our body hurts, it is usually because something *is* wrong with it— perhaps an infection or some change in body tissue. But with emotional discomfort, the pain is often because we *think* or *feel* there is something wrong, even when there isn't. This mistaken belief makes us self-conscious.

The logical solution is to achieve a true self-awareness. And there is no better way of doing this than by taking an inventory, which is the Fourth Step. Since we are apt to distort our observations about ourselves, we need an objective observer to help us, which is the Fifth Step.

When we discover our real self, we can feel normal without mind-altering chemicals.

Sober Judgment
❦

Alcohol and drugs are equal opportunity destroyers. They do not discriminate.

The phrase, "Sober as a judge" should not be taken literally. Judges are no more immune to chemical dependency than anyone else.

The reason the phrase came into usage is the obvious need for sobriety in order to issue a fair and responsible judgment. A good decision or judgment cannot be made when the brain is operating under the influence of a mind-altering chemical.

But judgments are not limited to the courtroom. We all make many judgments daily—judgments that affect not only our own lives but also the lives of others. Of greatest importance are people who are close to us, who are dependent upon us and may have no appeal from our judgments.

Being a judge is an awesome responsibility. The litigants are essentially at the mercy of the judge. But while there is a method of appeal if they feel the judge's decision is unfair, there is no appeal in our personal and family lives, where our judgments are, for all intents and purposes, final. Therefore, the responsibility is so much greater.

Responsible people are not reckless. Responsibility requires sobriety.

Healthy Dependencies
🍎

Some dependencies are healthy.

In planning the Gateway Rehabilitation Center, I met with my psychiatric colleagues and advised them that treatment would be oriented so that a person could make a smooth transition to AA or NA. Some psychiatrists objected. "All you're doing is taking the person's dependence off the bottle and putting it onto AA. You're not really treating the person's problem." Later that day I met with some people in AA, who said, "We alcoholics are dependent people. When we stop drinking, we take our dependency off the bottle and put it onto AA."

While both said the same thing, the psychiatrists were critical, as though they had some effective method of making people nondependent.

Dependency is a fact of life, not a trait unique to alcoholics. All humans are dependent in some way or other, and we all need one another to survive.

We do not have a choice whether or not to be dependent. Our only choice is between having a sick dependency or a healthy one. Chemicals are a sick dependency.

In recovery, we try to eliminate the sick dependencies and substitute healthy ones.

The Power of a Community

In recovery there is community.

I remarked to a director of a community mental health center that, while he may indeed have a mental health center, he does not have a community.

"What would you do if you suspected one of your clients was contemplating suicide?" I asked.

"We would send our crisis intervention team to the home," he replied.

"That is someone on your payroll," I said. "Suppose this were at two o'clock in the morning. Could you pull your crisis team together at that hour?"

"We could call the police to investigate," he said.

"That is another hired person on a payroll," I said.

"Just what are you getting at?" the mental health center director asked.

"Let me tell you what happens in addiction," I explained. "A call comes through at 2:00 A.M. that someone is in dire straits as a result of drinking. A person who is not being paid for his work will get up on a subzero night to help a total stranger, with full knowledge that if the caller had a change of mind, the volunteer can have the door slammed in his face at best or thrown down the stairs at worst. Yet he responds to the call."

Recovering people respond because of a sense of responsibility toward another human being, just as they had been helped. This sense of mutual responsibility is what constitutes a community.

Prescription for Tragedy
❦

There are danger zones in recovery.

For people recovering from chemical dependency, sobriety is indeed the most important focus of their lives. Without sobriety there can be no job, no family, no religion, no anything. Thus, sobriety must be guarded with the greatest zeal.

Yet various illnesses call for pain-killing medications that can jeopardize sobriety. This medication warrants serious consideration.

Doctors know that if a patient says, "I'm allergic to penicillin," they should not prescribe it. But if a patient says, "I'm alcoholic" or "I had a drug problem," not all doctors are aware that some drugs must be used with utmost caution. Too many people in recovery relapse as a result of well-intended medical treatment.

Recovering people must realize they are at risk if they use any mind-altering chemical. Have the treating physician consult a specialist on addictive disease, so as to plan a treatment that minimizes the risk of relapse. It is also important for the patient to notify his or her sponsor, so that contacts with support people in AA or NA can carry through this difficult period.

When appropriate precautions are taken, people in recovery can be adequately treated without risk of relapse.

Relapse and Re-entry

Relapse in chemical dependency is not uncommon.

If a person relapses early in recovery, there are usually many people who can help, because there are many people who have recovered after an early relapse.

But sometimes a person relapses after many years of sobriety, which presents an altogether different situation. This person may have had a solid recovery program and may have been sponsoring others, so returning to the recovery program is not easy. After all, we are apt to feel ashamed of relapsing, especially when others whom we had sponsored are sober. Furthermore, when we look for people who have relapsed after many years of sobriety and made a successful re-entry, they are not too plentiful.

Another problem in re-entry is that we may be looking for the same feeling we had when sobriety was novel. We are apt to be disappointed because there is only one "first kiss."

If we recognize addiction as a chronic disease that has been arrested, we can understand that vulnerability to relapse exists even after many years. Thus it is never safe to lose contact with the program. If a relapse should occur, neither we nor others who are sober should be judgmental. Finally, after we have regained sobriety following relapse, we should be available to help those who have a special problem of re-entry.

Couples Need to Recover Together
❧

Recovery sometimes generates new problems.

Sobriety is more than abstinence, which is only a state of inaction. It is a positive phenomenon with character growth and development.

When we become truly sober, we develop an entirely different life-style. True sobriety involves humility. It requires self-examination, frank admission of mistakes, and making amends to anyone we have offended. When we achieve true sobriety we become not only radically different from how we were during active use of chemicals but also different from how we were *before* we ever drank or used chemicals. Sobriety produces an entirely new personality.

If a spouse achieves sobriety and character growth, problems may occur when the nonchemically dependent partner does nothing about his or her own personality growth, either by involvement in Al-Anon or Nar-Anon, or through counseling. A disparity may develop, so that instead of everything getting better in the family when the addict recovers, new problems arise.

Just as we understand chemical dependency to be a family disease, we must realize that the recovery process is also a family recovery. Family programs can be helpful in enabling everyone to maximize individual character strengths and achieve growth.

Determination

The wisdom to know the difference.

Although we pray for courage to change those things that are amenable to change, we have blind spots and are sometimes unable to see that some things are changeable. Our impression may be that the challenge is too formidable, requiring extraordinary effort, or we may underestimate our abilities and consider ourselves incapable of succeeding. If we avoid a challenge which we are capable of overcoming, we are doing the very same thing we did in active addiction—the only difference now is that we employ avoidance without using a chemical.

Succeeding at anything requires a combination of human effort and Divine assistance. Courage is a character asset that we may be given if we ask for it. But it is possible for a courageous person to think, "Yes, I could do it, but why bother?" Having courage does not guarantee that we will make the effort. While we can pray to God to grant us courage, making the effort is *our* part of the job, not His.

Lessons Are Not Always Pleasant
🍃

"It is better to go to the house of a mourner than to a feast"—Ecclesiastes 7:2.

Why? Isn't a feast more pleasant?

Parties can be an escape from reality, and merriment is a way to divert our mind from problems. If not overdone, these escapes can serve a purpose. But for chemically dependent people, any such event must be without alcohol. Some people overdo partying and divert attention from too many realities. When problems are not addressed, they get worse.

Being in the house of a mourner may not be pleasant. People are sad, and there is the pain of those in grief. But this reminds us of our own mortality. We remember that if we wish to achieve something, there are limitations on the opportunities we have. We can't afford to squander time.

Ecclesiastes never said that it is more pleasant to be in the house of a mourner, but that it is *better*. Partying is more enjoyable, but it rarely stimulates anyone to greater achievement.

The Benefits of Fellowship
🍎

We talk least about things we think about the most.

The things that have the greatest effect on how we act are precisely those things we think about the most, because they relate to our deepest emotions. These are private matters, hardly the things we converse about. Yet because they are so secret, they are poorly defined. And because they are subject to distortion, they can have a detrimental influence on our behavior.

We may reveal these secrets to a therapist, but at one visit weekly this can be both a costly and a drawn-out process. Those who are fortunate enough to belong to a Twelve Step program can share these feelings with a sponsor or several intimate friends in the program, at no cost and at greater frequency.

I half jokingly suggest that if people outside the Twelve Step program only knew how much free therapy goes on at meetings, they might drink or use chemicals in order to qualify for membership. People who have already qualified are most foolish not to take full advantage of a fellowship that lets us talk about what we think.

Learn From the Past

Is history nothing more than a useless preoccupation with the past?

Reflecting on the past can be either constructive or destructive. Ruminating about something that cannot be undone, or indulging in remorse and guilt, is futile. It is like the child who cried because he dug a hole in the yard and could not bring it into the house. Since undoing the past is impossible, harping on it and flagellating ourselves does nothing except absorb scarce time and energy.

But looking at the mistakes of the past simply to avoid repeating them is constructive. Recognizing our vulnerabilities so that we may be on guard helps prevent repetition of errors. This reflection is not depressing because we look forward to positive achievements.

Memories are the key not to the past but to the future.

The Courage to Make the Right Change

❦

The Serenity Prayer has been reformulated in a variety of ways, often to clarify it.

For example, "The pessimist complains about the wind; the optimist expects it to change; the realist adjusts the sails."

Accepting that which cannot be changed is a job only half done. Even if we can accept with serenity, nothing may get accomplished. It is only when we accept with serenity and then go on to change what is changeable that progress is made.

Even if the pessimist accepted the wind with serenity, the ship would not be moved in the right direction. It will certainly not get there if we sit idly by and wait for the wind to change. The correct response is that of the realist, who accepts reality and makes the necessary adjustments.

Note that we do not pray to God to change things but, rather, to give us the courage to make the changes. We may indeed pray for the wind to change, but until it does so, we should adjust the sails.

Don't Make a Habit of Negativity

Dale Carnegie said, "Any fool can criticize, condemn, and complain—and most do."

Voice-sensitive computers can transform and convert sounds. It is feasible that there soon could be an apparatus to receive certain phrases and transform them, and broadcast them as "I am a fool."

But we don't have to look to exotic electronic devices to accomplish this. According to Dale Carnegie, when a person criticizes, condemns, and complains, he is making the public declaration, "I am a fool." Obviously, there are times when it is legitimate to do any of these, but when we do these together or habitually, our folly is revealed.

How often have we said about someone, "Why does he make such a fool of himself?" Of course, the person who is doing so is not aware of this. We should bear in mind that we are all vulnerable to such humiliation.

Fortunately, Carnegie has given us a way to avoid this: Don't criticize, condemn, or complain.

Flights of Fancy
🍎

A philosopher once said, "Think like a man of action, and act like a man of thought."

Science classifies humans as *Homo sapiens*, creatures with intellect. Although this is an incomplete definition of humans, it is undeniable that a unique characteristic is our intellect. To act without thinking is, therefore, being something less than fully human. Animals act according to whatever biological urge they have. We should first filter our urges through our mind, and select only those actions that are appropriate.

Just as it is important to act according to thought, we should also think according to our actions. Some people escape into fantasy, like a Walter Mitty, who lived in a make-believe world because he was dissatisfied with reality.

Chemical dependency and fantasy are both escapes from reality. While daydreaming is not toxic the way chemicals are, it can also be quite destructive if we so indulge in fantasy to neglect reality. Problems in the real world can be resolved only by taking action. Except for brief periods of innocent fantasy, we should limit our thoughts to what we can do.

See Yourself Through Someone Else

❦

Discovering character defects is not difficult—someone else's, that is.

In my book *Waking Up Just In Time*, I include a "Peanuts" strip showing Charlie Brown's class being taken to the woods for nature study. Sally asked Charlie, "What are we supposed to be doing here, anyway?" Charlie responds, "We're supposed to take notes." "Good!" says Sally, grabbing Charlie's tablet from him. "I'll take yours."

The Fourth of the Twelve Steps of recovery consists of taking a moral inventory. Some people have no problem taking this inventory because they take other people's inventories. It is quite simple to discover what everyone else is doing wrong, but rather difficult to pinpoint our own defective behavior. Our rationalization capacities work overtime to justify everything we do.

Because we are blind to our own defects, we must enlist the assistance of a trusted friend who cares enough to point out our defects to us.

Trust

Trust is essential to any meaningful relationship.

Trust is not always easy to come by. Some people have been deeply hurt because others violated their trust. In order to protect themselves from further injury, they no longer trust anyone. Some people say that even when they trusted in God, they were disappointed because He did not come through for them as expected. Absence of all trust, however, results in a loneliness that can be intolerable and may actually contribute to recourse to chemicals.

How can you learn to trust again? The first step is to learn that trust does exist. Allow someone to trust you, and guard that trust zealously. Once you know by virtue of your own experience that trust does exist, you can cautiously begin to trust others. You cannot be the only person in the world who possesses trust. Explore who else does.

Self-Reproach Can Be Deceptive
❧

Self-reproach is not always a virtue.

Criticizing ourselves for wrongful behavior can be constructive if it results in our avoiding its repetition. But sometimes we criticize ourselves for less than sincere reasons. For instance, we may jump the gun and chastise ourselves before someone else has the opportunity to do so. This is self-protection, not self-correction.

Recovery frowns on the "pity party." This is not necessarily feeling sorry for ourselves for adversities, but rather a self-flagellation by which we elicit sympathy and ward off criticism from others. As children we may have learned to anticipate a scolding and volunteer, "I've been bad today." Our parents would then say, "There, there. It's not all that terrible." As adults we repeat this juvenile behavior.

The Fifth Step requires a sincere admission. A trained Fifth Step listener can alert us if we are deceiving ourselves with self-reproach.

Our Animal Instincts

A gentleman in recovery said, "My ego cries for perfection, but honesty tells me that I am human, that humanity is not so terrible, and that it's okay to be half child of God and half s.o.b."

We are comprised of flesh and blood. We have virtually all the impulses, drives, and desires that animals have, including greed, hostility, and lust. But we differ from animals in that we have the capacity to be masters over ourselves, and do only that which befits us as human beings. When we achieve this mastery, then we are, as the man describes, half child of God—in that we control our behavior—and half s.o.b.—the latter half being the animal part of us.

There's nothing much we can do about the animal part of us; it is rooted in our biology. We can control our animal half, but we cannot eradicate it. But that does not mean that it cannot be removed. The One who put it there has the ability to remove it.

When we have done everything within our power to achieve mastery over our biological drives, we can ask God to remove those character traits that we feel are undesirable. God may indeed do so—or it may be His will for us to continue the struggle, because as we struggle to achieve and maintain mastery, we grow in character and spirituality.

Overindulgence

All addictive diseases—alcohol, drugs, food, gambling, or sex—are diseases of excess.

Why do animals in their natural habitat not indulge to excess? When animals satisfy their nutritional needs, they stop eating. When they satisfy their sexual drive, they stop. Why are only humans subject to excess? Why do all people not have the normal physiological endpoint to limit their drives?

Perhaps it is because there is one drive in the human being that does not have an endpoint—the drive for spiritual growth. The capacity to grow spiritually is indeed infinite; it *has* no endpoint.

Some people do not recognize their need for spiritual growth. They try to quell their spiritual craving by indulging in food, alcohol, drugs, sex or riches. None of these can even begin to fill the spiritual void. They are like trying to fill a bottomless pit; the attempt frustrates our true needs. A recovering person said it so well. "When I stopped drinking, I discovered there was a void within me. There was an empty space, and that was the space where God belonged."

All indulgences are inappropriate. Growing in spirituality can give us the satisfaction we crave, and allow us to avoid the diseases of indulgence.

Why Deaden Your Feelings?
❦

Mood-altering substances alter a person's physical or emotional pain.

Is it possible that some people have greater recourse to chemicals because they *feel* more intensely than others? While it is likely that some nonchemically dependent people have more effective ways of coping with distressing feelings, is it not possible that some nonaddicts do not feel as deeply or intensely and are actually less sensitive?

Some addicted people indeed *do* feel more intensely, and this holds true for all feelings—pain, love, envy, hate, joy, pride, or compassion. When the addict recovers and abstains, what happens to those intense feelings? The person learns how to handle them without recourse to chemicals, but the *intensity* of the feeling mechanism does not change. In any group of recovering addicts, there are likely to be more highly sensitive and "deep-feeling" people than in a comparable group of nonchemically dependent people.

So if you are a recovering person, you have paid a price for your heightened emotional sensitivity. You probably are hurt more easily and feel pain more intensely. However, these feelings make you so much more human, more interesting, and more lovable.

The Price of Self-Knowledge
🍎

Some people shudder at the thought of being an addict.

Sometimes they cannot even get themselves to pronounce the word. I often say to the newcomer, "Today you think that being an addict is absolutely terrible, the worst thing that has ever happened to you. But after one year of sobriety, you will discover that it is not so terrible to be an addict.

"Perhaps after two years you will say, 'My name is Jane Doe and I am a grateful addict,' meaning that you are grateful for your recovery. Some time after that you will again say, 'I am a grateful addict,' but this time you will mean that you are grateful for *being* an addict. Because by then you will have realized that your growth in personality and spirituality could never have been attained without going through addiction and recovery."

Few nonaddicts take a personal moral inventory, and still fewer bare their souls to another person. Consequently, few people ever achieve a self-awareness. Many people live their entire lives without ever knowing who they are. It is only when a crisis such as chemical dependency forces a person into a self-analysis that self-awareness is achieved.

Perhaps being an addict is a high price to pay for self-awareness, but things that are truly precious and valuable do not come cheap.

Encounter With a Stranger
🍎

A young man admitted for chemical dependency confided harboring suicidal thoughts. "Suppose you had carried out your intention," I asked. "Just whom would you have killed?"

"Myself, of course," the man answered.

"Let me give you two examples of criminal homicide," I said. "The first is that of a man who is furious with someone who had intentionally harmed him, and he kills this person. While criminal, such a thing is understandable.

"The other example is a person who goes into a supermarket and shoots people at random. This is not only criminal but completely insane. What is it that makes the person in this second case so crazy?" I asked.

"Well, this guy must be crazy to go around killing total strangers," the man answered.

"Exactly," I said. "Now tell me, do you really know yourself?"

"I guess not," the man answered.

"Then how could you possibly consider suicide? It would be totally *insane* for you to kill someone you don't even know."

Suicidal thoughts are not infrequent among chemically dependent people. Without exception, we are people who never really knew ourselves. Thus, a major part of our recovery consists of getting to know ourselves.

Pray for the Courage to Change
❦

"If the mind doesn't come, just bring the body."

Newcomers to recovery may say that the meetings do not touch them emotionally. They are told, "You don't have to understand the program to benefit from it. If your mind is not registering, don't panic. Mind involvement is not essential for recovery at this point. Just bring your body to these meetings."

While mind involvement is *crucial* for recovery, it frequently is not there at the beginning, and comes only after an extended period of time. But if we persist long enough, then even if *we* don't get the program, *it* gets *us*.

There are reasons for the mind to not engage initially. We still show denial and resistance to considering ourselves addicted, we fear giving up chemicals forever, and we fear *change*. Sobriety requires not only abstinence but changes in attitude, behavior, priorities, and friends. Change is something we inherently resist.

The concept of change is important to the veteran in sobriety as well as the neophyte. It is easy to become complacent after several years of abstinence, and to think that we have already made all the essential changes. Obviously, this is not true. Why else do we still say the Serenity Prayer? Why else do we pray for the *courage* to change?

Move Beyond Self-Pity
❦

One of the pitfalls in addiction is self-pity.

If we indulge in self-pity, we are not likely to stop chemical use. If we have abstained and we begin to feel sorry for ourselves, we are likely to relapse.

Self-pity is the result of feeling short-changed. "The world has not been nice to me, and has not given me my just desserts." This is based on the assumption that there is something we deserve of which we have been deprived.

What if the world was *not* created to be our amusement park? What if everything in the world was *not* put there just to serve our needs? What if it is just the other way around—that we were put here to do something for the world? The emphasis shifts completely. No one owes us anything. It is we who are obligated, and we owe the world something.

Seeking to do God's will is the realization that we are here to do a job rather than to enjoy ourselves. This idea helps avoid self-pity. We are not deprived of anything. We are here to do the work in the bidding of the Higher Power.

We pray to be shown the will of God because, if we forget what we are really here for, we begin thinking we were created to enjoy everything. And when we lack enjoyment or suffer distress, we feel sorry for ourselves—and then come the chemicals to compensate.

Sobriety requires an attitude that we are to be givers rather than takers.

Helping Others Understand
Our Changes
❧

Recovery is a new birth, and means adapting to a new person.

A young woman who had been separated from her newly recovering husband was considering reconciliation. Although she said she had lost all feeling for him, it was obvious that she wished to consider the possibility of a relationship.

I suggested that rather than think in terms of reconciliation, she date this man as if she were getting to know a total stranger. This new person not only bears no resemblance to the addicted person she knew but also has no resemblance to the person *before* he used chemicals or drank.

Recovery is not a quick process. The person who will emerge from this process is totally unknown.

To people who knew the active addict, this may be bewildering. But they can get help and insight by participating in family therapy and in Al-Anon family groups. Should they decide not to reestablish the relationship, the experience and personal growth of participating in one of these programs is extremely valuable.

The addict has no option but to change and grow, because his very life depends on it. Participation in the family program can provide the opportunity to understand the recovering person.

Be Receptive to the Truth

We should keep our sense keenly alert.

A recovering person told me, "It was what you said to me that one day turned me around." Yet what I had said was neither unusual nor profound.

Jim is a young man who was admitted for his fourth detox at about 3:00 A.M. When I saw him at 8:00 A.M., he was still very intoxicated. I said, "Jim, go back to your room and sleep it off. I'll talk to you later."

Two years later, after two years of sobriety, Jim described his last admission at an AA meeting, saying that on the way back to his room that morning, he said to himself, "My God, I am so drunk and in such terrible shape that Abe can't even talk to me." He then went to his room, fell to his knees, and for the first time said, "God, help me now!"

Obviously, there was nothing profound about what I had said. The reason my comment impacted on Jim was that he was receptive to hearing what he had not been able to hear before.

How many things might we be overlooking today because we are not receptive?

We can only pray that we are able to see and hear the truth. We also must overcome our stubbornness and consider the possibility that we may be mistaken—that other people's observations might be right.

Wisdom and Experience

The ideal combination: the energy of youth and the wisdom of experience.

Ethel was thirty-four on her eighth admission for withdrawal from heroin—prior to the time of treatment centers and NA. She confronted me angrily, "How can you believe in God? If there was a just God, would he allow you to do something when you're not old enough to know better and be cursed because of it for the rest of your life?

"What did I know when I was sixteen and a guy shoved a needle in my arm? The first year was fun, but ever since it has been hell. I don't have the guts to kill myself and I'm not lucky enough to overdose the way some of my friends did."

We may indeed question why we have our greatest wisdom when we are at retirement age and need it least. For some reason, maximum energy and maximum wisdom are incompatible. The Divine plan is for energetic youth to be guided by its wiser elders. Too bad this plan is not widely implemented.

Seeing Our Faults in Others

Projection is a psychological maneuver whereby we see our own defects in other people.

In the "Peanuts" comic strip, Lucy considers herself superior to everyone else. Lucy looks at some little bugs, and shouts at one of them, "What makes you think you're better than all the other bugs?" Then she walks away saying, "Bugs like that have to be put in their place." No one can really know what any bug thinks, but Lucy knows this for certain because what Lucy really sees is herself.

Projection can be a guideline for self-improvement. Anytime we see a fault in someone else, this should alert us that we may be projecting. What we have discovered in others really may not exist in them at all, but rather be in ourselves.

How wonderful the world would be if every time we felt like criticizing others we stopped and did a careful self-evaluation. We would at least delay our critical remarks, and we would come to a more thorough self-awareness.

Empathy
❦

Our understanding of what *is* depends on how deeply we feel.

Toward the close of Yom Kippur, a rabbi conducted an appeal for funds for the needy. This was a day on which all the congregants observed a 24-hour deprivation of food and water. "Now that you are hungry," he said, "you can better appreciate the needs of those who have no food, and contribute accordingly."

When our stomachs are full, we can appease our conscience with small donations. But if we identify with the hungry, we are likely to be more generous.

To deal fairly and justly with people, we must empathize with them. It is this empathy that enables one addict to help another. The same empathy should operate among all humans, addicted or nonaddicted.

Legal Drugs are Just as Lethal
❧

Medical addiction is no less serious than street addiction.

Chemical dependency may result from medication prescribed by a doctor for pain, insomnia, or anxiety. It is not known why some people develop a dependency on prescribed medications and others do not.

When a person uses addictive-type medications for chronic symptoms, the effectiveness of the dose gradually decreases. The person then uses larger doses for relief of the symptoms. Eventually the symptoms break through even massive doses, so that the suffering person now has an addiction superimposed upon the original symptoms. Treatment for medically induced addiction can be more difficult than for other types, but once the addiction is identified and the patient makes a commitment to recover, treatment is feasible.

The recovery program, which works so well in helping people cope with stress without resorting to chemicals, can also help the medication addict cope with the discomfort of pain.

Keep Pain in Perspective
❦

The degree of discomfort we feel is not an objective phenomenon.

A young woman in early recovery complained of having had a very depressing day, but observation indicated that she was less depressed than previously. The reason she felt more depressed was that she had experienced several good days.

If we fall from a ladder, the severity of the fall depends on which rung we were standing on. A fall from the first rung may not cause any pain, whereas a fall from the eighth rung may be very painful. A depressing day after several other depressing days is not felt as deeply as a less depressing day that follows a sequence of good days.

Recovery tends to take a zig-zag course rather than make a smooth upward progression. When several good days are followed by an off day, do not panic. The fact that they feel so painful actually may be because you are at a higher level of recovery. That greater discomfort may be a sign of healing.

Our Purpose in Life

Too often we identify ourselves by what we *do* rather than by what we *are*.

The primary purpose of an occupation is to provide the means for survival. Unless we have some ultimate purpose, however, we work to survive in order to work—which is a meaningless cycle.

How can we know *what* we are? By looking at what we do during our nonworking hours, when we are not engaged in the means for survival. It might be shocking to discover that our ultimate purpose in life is to watch television or lose ourselves in some other diversion.

Rest and relaxation are as vital to life as food and water. But after all our vital necessities have been met, there should be something for which we live. If we do not have an ultimate goal, we should at least be occupied in looking for one.

Avoid the Superficial

Outward appearances may be impressive, but they are not an indication of value.

We are often impressed by what we see, and we may be envious of others. How surprised we would be to discover that those we envy may be envious of us!

We are often dissatisfied by our lot in life because we compare ourselves to others. It has been said that if everyone's life were put in a see-through container, and we had the freedom to choose, we would all choose our own life.

Roses are certainly prettier than cabbages and much more fragrant, but cabbages make far better soup. If all we want is color and fragrance, we should go for the roses. But then we must be ready to accept pretty, sweet-smelling starvation.

The real values in life lie in substance and content, not in appearances.

Arrogance and Error
🍎

To err is human, but what about making a mistake?

It is widely assumed that *error* and *mistake* are synonymous. It was, therefore, enlightening to come across the statement, "An error doesn't become a mistake until you refuse to correct it." According to this, to err is human because no one is perfect. The same leniency cannot be extended to a mistake, because everyone has the capacity to rectify an error, or at least to try.

Although we cannot justify a wrong act resulting from yielding to temptation, there is at least a partial defense—that we lacked the strength to resist. However, once the act is over and the temptation has been satisfied, what defense can there be for not trying to rectify a wrong? The only obstacle is our ego, which may not allow us to admit having done wrong. Such arrogance is the worst possible character defect.

In recovery we learn humility and the need to make amends, because both go together. If we can admit being in error, we can avoid all mistakes.

Don't Live Only in the Present
🍂

"One day at a time" does not mean to live just for the present moment.

Digital clocks have become very popular, perhaps because they represent a cultural attitude. The pointers on a clock's face indicate the present time, but the present and future can be seen as well. A digital clock has no past and no future, only the now.

When society rejects the traditions of the past, and exploits natural resources so as to endanger its future, the concern is only with the present. Ours is a digital clock generation.

Chemical addiction is just another manifestation of preoccupation with the present. Cherished values of the past are rejected and serious dangers for the future are ignored. The momentary high is all that counts.

In recovery we discover how destructive this narrow perspective is, and we change our attitudes. What the world needs is a recovery program to overcome this addictive attention to the present.

Treat Your Body With Respect
❦

Every human being merits respect.

A person is composed of a physical body that houses a divine soul. The body is thus a temple that contains the Divine, and as such should be accorded its due honor.

The body must be treated with dignity. Even the lifeless body must be handled respectfully. How much more so must the living body be respected.

Just as it is forbidden to injure the body of another person, it is forbidden to injure ourselves. Our bodies are not our exclusive property to do with what we wish. They are instruments wherewith to experience life. They were entrusted to us by God in order that we can fulfill our mission on earth.

It is forbidden to introduce harmful chemicals that ruin or deface the body. The body is a sacred object that must be accorded due reverence.

Just as sobriety restores respect for the body so that we no longer deface it, it must also restore the dignity of the body's actions. And our behavior must reflect the sanctity of the human being.

Concern For the Common Good

We must respect the rights of others, just as we do our own.

The Talmud tells of a man who was clearing his yard and throwing rocks into the street. A wise man rebuked him, "Why do you throw things from someone else's property into your own?" The rebuke was dismissed with derision.

Sometime later the man went bankrupt and lost his property. Walking along the street, he stumbled on one of the rocks he had thrown out. "How wise was the man who rebuked me," he said. "It is the street that is really my permanent property."

We may selfishly think that what we own is ours forever. The only thing that is truly ours is that which we share with the rest of the world, for that cannot be taken from us.

It is the common good that is our own good. If we injure anything or anyone in the world, we are really injuring ourselves.

Learn From Others' Hindsight
☙

Many people get their priorities in order—too late.

During my tenure as rabbi, I had many opportunities to be with people during the last few days of their lives. As they reviewed their lives some said, "I really regret that I did not spend more time with my family." Or "I regret that I did not come to religious services more often." Never did anyone say, "I regret I did not spend more time at the office."

Not too often can we profit from our own hindsight, but we can certainly take advantage of other people's hindsight and use it as our *fore*sight.

In recovery from chemical dependency we have learned how unwise it is to favor immediate gratification over long-term consequences.

If we put these two ideas together, we can live our lives in such a manner that we will have few regrets.

Distorted Judgment

How can we divest ourselves of resentment?

If we think back on some of the things we did during active addiction, we find some regrets. We certainly did not intend the injuries that occurred. On some occasions we had been warned not to do something, but in our state of mind it appeared to be the right thing.

Because our judgment had been distorted by chemicals, we did unwise things—not because we were bad, but because we did not know better.

Use of chemicals is not the only way our judgment can be distorted. All kinds of ideas and emotions interact to bring about judgment. Many of the people who provoke us are acting under distortions of judgment. They may have no intention of harming or offending us.

We feel sorry for them, just as we do for someone behaving destructively under the influence of chemicals. But if we can't manage to feel sorry for people who suffer from distortion of judgment, at least we can refrain from hating them.

Stay in Control

Surrender need not be a bad word.

Some machines have both automatic and manual controls. If the automatic fails, the machine can be operated by manual control.

Many people have an automatic control in the brain that shuts off the desire for mind-altering chemicals. For example, they will not take more than one or two drinks. But in other people, the automatic control is not operative, and they must use manual control.

Our manual control system is ineffective. Most people are unaware of this because their automatic system functions well. But when it doesn't, and we try to use an ineffective manual system, trouble invariably results.

If the automatic controls cannot be repaired, the only solution is to improve the manual. This is what we do when we join a recovery fellowship. We do not really give up control—we just improve whatever control is available.

Surrender does not mean we must "say uncle." It means only that the automatic system is out of commission and we must strengthen the manual control.

Are You Open to New Ideas?
🌱

It is always possible to learn something new.

Every day we are bombarded by new things. Yet if we were to reckon every night what new knowledge we acquired that day, we might be surprised to discover we learned nothing new.

How can this be? If we are surrounded by knowledge, why can we not point to several new things we learned? There is only one answer: the knowledge was there but we failed to absorb it. We did not *try* to learn. Why? Probably because we feel we already know enough. "A fool is better off than someone who considers himself wise"—Proverbs 26:12. A fool may be open to learning, whereas someone who thinks himself wise will never learn anything.

People with years of quality sobriety state, "There has never been a meeting at which I didn't gain something." People who abandon the program say, "There was no point in going to meetings. It was the same thing over and over again."

The former are open to learning, the latter are not.

Can You Be Alone With Yourself?
❦

Solitude and loneliness are diametric opposites.

Solitude can be pleasant. We may seek to be free of all distractions and pressures in order to be alone with ourselves, to relax or meditate. Solitude can be invigorating. It allows us to return to normal activities and associations with greater strength.

Loneliness is painful, perhaps the most painful sensation known to humankind. Lonely people can be desperate and may take radical action to escape their loneliness. They invite distractions of any type to banish their feelings of loneliness. Many people have resorted to chemicals in order to escape from loneliness.

The difference between solitude and loneliness is that in solitude we have *ourselves* and are comfortable being with ourselves. The lonely person has no self, or has a self that is despised. The lonely person cannot tolerate being with either a despised self or in a state of nothingness.

Recovery and fellowship are effective not merely because they provides the companionship of other people. The recovery program helps us discover the true self—someone who can be not only tolerated but actually enjoyed.

Learning From Each Other
❦

We need old friends to help us grow old, and new friends to help us stay young.

Not too many people have the opportunity to befriend people of all ages. Young people tend to associate with their peers, and older folks with theirs. The latter may indeed grow old together, but depression sets in when the group thins out by attrition.

The recovery program provides an unparalleled opportunity to avoid this. People of all ages attend meetings. And because it is generally the oldest members who have the most years of sobriety, young people are advised to seek their advice or engage them as sponsors. The young benefit from the experience and wisdom of the old. And the older people are rejuvenated by their association with the young, reliving experiences they had decades ago. The program is always replenished with newcomers. The old are always needed, and never outgrow their usefulness.

Perhaps the program is not the proverbial fountain of youth, but it is certainly a far cry from a depressing assemblage of people who feel that life is behind them.

Dreamers and Doers

The Serenity Prayer is well formulated.

It might have read, "God grant me the courage to change that which I can and the serenity to accept that which I cannot change." Note that acceptance of the unchangeable comes first.

A recovering person remarked, "Once I accept things as they are, I can create things as they might be." Great inventors and explorers had dreams that led them to their achievements. Yet few daydreamers are inventors or explorers, because people who live in a world of fantasy, like James Thurber's Walter Mitty, cannot accomplish anything. It is only if we have a firm basis in reality, accepting it for what it is, that we can make changes.

Columbus did not resign himself to a flat world. He had the courage to change attitudes, with the knowledge and skill to bring it about. That is how we must approach life.

The Treasure Within

If happiness is anywhere, it is within ourselves.

There is a legend about a man who dreamt repeatedly that there was a treasure buried at the foot of a bridge in a distant city. He traveled to the city and, when he began digging, he was stopped by a police officer. When the man explained why he was digging, the officer laughed. "How foolish," he said. "Why, I have dreamt that in a distant village there is a little hut under which is buried a huge treasure." The man realized that this was his own hut, and upon returning home, dug and found the treasure.

Our quest for happiness can take us to the four corners of the world, to different relationships, to various occupations—or to chemicals.

Why engage in a fruitless search? Ask people who have tried everything, and they will tell you. We may be so busy looking for a treasure elsewhere that we fail to discover it where it really is—within ourselves.

The Emptiness of an Unexamined Life
🍂

Voltaire said that doubt is not a pleasant state, but that certainty is a ridiculous one.

Voltaire was criticizing the person who refuses to submit to critical analysis. Although I am certain I write with a pen, I have no objection to anyone who wishes to examine whether it really is a pen. I do not object to this examination precisely because I am certain of the fact.

However, there are certainties we refuse to examine—beliefs about which we are so positive that we do not subject them to critical analysis. But life is anything but certain. We are defensive and fear that such analysis will prove our belief to be untrue.

The active addict refuses to submit to evaluation. He is certain he is *not* addicted. It is this kind of certainty that is indeed ridiculous.

Infantile Amusements

"When I grow up, I want to be a child."

This statement was not made by a child, because children dream of becoming adults. It was made by a grown-up who recalled the freedom from worry and stress that characterized childhood.

Children want to be big because they see themselves as tiny and powerless. Grown-ups have authority and power. Yet grown-ups crave the carefree spirit of childhood, and would gladly yield their greater size and stature to be free of the responsibilities and burdens of adulthood.

While our intellect tells us that we can never be children again, our hearts long for the fabled fountain of youth. Our entertainment industry is nothing but a sophisticated version of childhood play.

Our intellect must triumph, however, and we must assume the serious business of life. We can be amused and we can distract ourselves with entertainments, but these activities should not become our goals in life.

Can an Addict Be Honest?
❦

For many people, truth is a virtue; for people in recovery, it is life saving.

In addition to use of chemicals, addiction is characterized by certain behavior patterns, foremost among which is lying. No one has ever maintained truthfulness while being an addict.

Just as the first drink or drug can be the beginning of a full-blown relapse, so can the first lie set the addictive pattern into motion. We must be as cautious about lying as we are about using a chemical.

Lying can generally be avoided if we resolve never to do anything that we might later have to deny. This dedication to truthfulness yields rich dividends, because not only does it eliminate the need to lie but it also avoids doing things that we might wish to conceal.

This is why the recovery program insists on rigorous honesty. It cites the "inability to be honest" as the factor most responsible for a failure to recover.

Turn Down the Volume
🍎

The fewer the facts, the stronger the opinion.

A politician had just finished his speech and left the text on the lectern. In the margin he had made notations to guide his delivery: "slow," "gesticulate," and so on. At one point there was a note, "Argument awfully weak here. Scream like hell!"

Good arguments do not require many decibels to be heard. The strength of an argument is enough to carry it. It is only when the argument is weak that we yell loudly, trying to impress others with sound what is lacking in content. For example, I have never heard anyone yell, "I am an alcoholic." But I have certainly heard very loud protests, "I am *not* an alcoholic."

Attention to the loudness of an assertion can help us gauge its validity. Similarly, if you find yourself yelling, whether at home, at work, or with friends, pause and reflect. If what you're saying is really correct, there should be no need for screaming. Furthermore, if you are speaking in a loud and explosive manner, it deflects from your message. If you wish to be heard, speak softly.

Insults and Criticism
❦

When is criticism constructive?

Sometimes we point out a character defect or a mistake to someone, and all we really are doing is insulting or belittling the person. At other times, the same message is helpful criticism. How can we distinguish between the two, as both givers and receivers of criticism?

There is a simple rule. If the person who criticizes is willing to help correct a mistake, it is sincere and constructive criticism. If the person just makes a critical comment and then walks away, it is an insult.

Many people in recovery point out what you are doing wrong, but they are ready to take time and share their knowledge and experience so that you can rectify the defect or mistake. These are the people who should be heeded. But if someone preaches to you and walks away, consider what was said but do not consider this person a friend.

If you find yourself tempted to point out to someone what he or she is doing wrong, stop and reflect. Are you willing to help correct that behavior? If not, hold your peace.

Faith and Reason

When we feel our faith challenged, we may think, "If only we could see God, we could be so sure."

DeSaint-Exupery said, "It is only with the heart that one can see rightly; what is essential is invisible to the eye."

Contrary to popular assumption, seeing is *not* believing. We believe only in that which we do not see. But of the two, which is the stronger, and which is most important to people?

Thousands of people have given their lives for what they believe, but there is no record of anyone sacrificing his life for what he saw. A person who readily accepts martyrdom rather than deny the God in whom he believes has no trouble denying that two plus two equals four if this will save his life. While proven facts are important, they rarely inspire people the way belief does.

Faith is an internal knowledge, a kind of intuition, a wisdom of the heart that is in some way superior to the wisdom of the brain. More people have been inspired to sobriety by faith than by scientific fact.

Don't Fight Success

Sobriety is not a philosophical concept.

An attorney with twenty-five years of sobriety related how his first experiences with AA resulted in repeated relapses. He asked a seasoned veteran what he was doing wrong, and was told that his error was trying to *understand* the program. "Just listen and do as you're told." The young man was enraged and insulted. "I am not an imbecile. I am a thinking person, and I must understand why I do something.

"I later reflected that all my understanding is getting me drunk, while this other person is staying sober. I therefore elected to experiment by listening and following instructions for just a short period of time, and here I am, twenty-five years sober."

It has been wisely said, "Let no one be deluded that a knowledge of the path can substitute for putting one foot in front of the other."

Sobriety is achieved by doing, not by thinking.

Learn From Your Mistakes
❦

God created humans, but human beings continue to create themselves.

People are complex organisms, composed of genes that constitute the past; impressions of the environment which include our parents, teachers, and friends; and our own actions. There may not be much we can do about the first two components, but our actions are within our domain—to do or not to do.

The writer Oscar Wilde said, "It is not what one does that is wrong, but what one becomes as a consequence of it." Anything we do does not remain external to us, but becomes part of our character. A good deed makes us better, and a bad deed makes us worse.

The changes that our actions make in ourselves are not cast in stone and can be undone. This is why amends work and why they are necessary. Unless we make amends, we allow the effects that a wrong act had on our personality to remain. Even though we would not repeat these wrong acts, it is as though we served delicious food with dirty hands. Making amends is a cleansing process.

Whatever we were created is the raw material of which we are made. With our actions we fashion ourselves into the ultimate object.

We Are Alike But Not the Same
❦

We are not unique, yet we are unique.

One of the pitfalls in recovery is the idea "I'm different." If we think that the principles in recovery apply only to others, and that we are exempt from following these because we are different, trouble is sure to follow. "I don't need all those meetings. I don't need a sponsor. I can take an occasional drink. Yes, I am an alcoholic or addict, but I am different." These ideas are guaranteed to result in relapse.

Yet every person is unique. Our fingerprints are different, our facial features are different, our voices are different, and no two people think identically. The columnist George Will said, "It is extraordinary how extraordinary the ordinary person is."

If a million keys are made of the same metal, they are all alike in substance, but only one will work in a given lock. As far as our addiction is concerned, we are all alike, and the rules of recovery apply equally to everyone. But as far as our mission in life is concerned, we are unique. "I turn my life over to the will of God for me, because whatever He wishes me to do is my personal assignment. In that way I am extraordinary, and no one else can do that which I am supposed to do."

Being unique is a responsibility to be zealously guarded.

Get Sober: You Deserve It

Recovery must be for ourselves.

A young woman was admitted for treatment of drug addiction. She had been abstinent on several occasions for a maximum of five months. "I was sober for my parents, for my children, and for my friends, but I was never sober for myself," she said, bursting into tears.

It was not difficult to surmise why this woman had not been able to be sober for herself. This "self" as she perceived it was not deserving of sacrifice. There was no reason to do anything for this "worthless" self.

Another young woman said, "I gave myself totally to my children, but so what? A total gift of nothing is still nothing."

Self-esteem is pivotal in recovery. Not only will people with self-confidence have no need to escape from reality, but they will also endure any discomforts of abstinence for their own sake—just as many people are ready to do for the sake of others.

One of the reasons sobriety for others' sake does not work is that others are not always around. In absence of the stimulus for abstinence, relapse may occur. The self, however, is *always* there, and recovery for oneself can be permanent.

Keep it Simple

People who have difficulty with the Twelve Step program are unusual indeed.

Sometimes it requires an unusual mind to undertake an analysis of the obvious. What could be more obvious than, "If you don't take the first drink you won't get drunk?" What is there to analyze about this?

A recovering alcoholic with forty years of sobriety was asked for his secret. His answer: "Don't drink and don't die." What could be more simple?

Analysis means dissecting something into its component parts. We can only analyze something complex, because something absolutely simple doesn't have any components. A compound can be broken down into its elements, but an element cannot be analyzed. Imagine, then, the frustration we experience in trying to analyze the recovery program, one of whose axioms is "Keep it simple!"

The beauty of the Twelve Step program is its utter simplicity. Only an unusual mind would try to analyze it.

Miracles Can Happen

Higher Power awareness can occur in different ways.

A recovering biologist said, "I was looking through a microscope at a fertilized ovum, and it struck me that the only addition to that cell during the next nine months would be nutrients—proteins, fats, carbohydrates, and water—none of which can think or feel. Within this single tiny cell, then, lies the capacity of thought and feeling and creativity: to compose a great symphony, to write a masterpiece of literature, or to discover a life-saving procedure. It was at that moment that I discovered God. Strange, this never occurred to me all the years that I drank."

Miracles occur all around us. Nature is nothing but a series of miracles that occur with such regularity they are taken for granted. We can look at a phenomenon and easily recognize its miraculous character, or we can look at the regularity and conclude that things happen on their own. Chemicals result in the latter kind of thinking, whereas sobriety cleanses the mind and allows it to perceive the truth.

Once we recognize the miracle of sobriety, it is much easier to see miracles everywhere.

Putting God in Charge

Why is belief in a Higher Power necessary for recovery?

All challenges in life can be divided into three simple categories: 1. those that are impossible; 2. those that are possible for one to do unassisted; and 3. those that one can do with some help.

People with inflated egos—who consider asking for help to be demeaning and an admission of weakness—dismiss the third group as nonexistent. For them, reality consists either of the impossible or that which they can do themselves. As a result, they either give up on things that could be accomplished with help or foolishly tackle things alone that are beyond their capacity.

Enlisting the help of a Higher Power, whatever we wish that to be, puts reality back into proper perspective. This is an essential ingredient of recovery. Of course, when we accept this and relinquish the fantasy that we are our own highest power, the concept of *God as I understand Him* becomes feasible.

From Mirage to Reality
❦

Addiction is a mirage; sobriety is real.

A person who sees a mirage is certain of what she sees until she reaches it and discovers it to be nothing but a hallucination. The person who sets out toward sobriety may not see the goal, and may not even have a concept of what it will be like to be sober, but the goal is real nevertheless.

A veteran recovering alcohol addict described the first steps in recovery as someone standing at a river's edge waiting to get across, and is told to start rowing. "But there is no boat," he protests. "Never mind!" he is told. "Just begin rowing. The boat will appear."

This may sound absurd, but what is meant is that when we begin working the program, we may have no idea of either the vehicle or the goal of recovery, but if we begin to make the effort, both will appear.

We can well understand the anxiety and bewilderment at being told to begin rowing when we do not see a boat. But when scores of people assure us that as we begin to row the boat will appear and we can safely cross the river—and when such assurance is based on abundant personal experience—we gather the courage to begin rowing. The sobriety boat indeed appears.

Keep Your Mind Open
🍒

The mind is the essence of a person.

Whereas we must remember our mistakes in order to rectify them, once we have taken adequate corrective action, the incident should be put out of mind. Ruminating on it constitutes reliving the experience.

Two Buddhist monks encountered a woman who was unable to wade across a creek. One monk lifted her and carried her across. Sometime later his comrade asked, "Why did you violate our rules and have physical contact with a woman?" The first monk replied, "I put her down two miles back, but you are still carrying her."

Our minds are creative instruments by which we receive data, analyze them, synthesize them, and formulate what we wish to do. The mind cannot operate at optimum efficiency if it is encumbered by baggage of the past. Unpleasant events that linger have a negative influence on the function of the mind.

A refusal to let go of the past impedes working with the present and toward the future. If any past actions have injured someone, we must indeed make amends, but then we must let go. Wherever our mind is, that is where our person is.

Living a Lie
🍂

Lying is as impractical as it is immoral.

The human brain is a super computer. It has a vast memory bank that can store vast amounts of information. However, even this memory bank has its limitations. As with any computer, it is possible for its capacity to be exhausted.

Facts require little retention. A tree was a tree ten years ago, is a tree today, and will be a tree ten years hence. Falsehoods, however, have no existence in reality, and must be retained in memory. A faulty memory will, of course, soon expose the false nature of a statement.

Even if memory is intact, the storage of falsehoods occupies precious space where truth could be stored. Retention of these falsehoods will, therefore, diminish the brain's capacity to store useful information. While we may deceive another person with a lie, we cannot make constructive use of false information.

Truthfulness cannot be maintained during active addiction. Excuses, cover-ups, and frank distortion of fact characterize addiction. Many recovering people have expressed a sense of relief that they no longer need to tax their memories. Some have said that the euphoria of early sobriety comes from casting off the burden of living a falsehood.

To live a lie is not only unethical, but also stupid.

Grasp One Small Thing at a Time
🍂

"One day at a time" is not an AA brainchild.

Leonardo da Vinci, one of the world's geniuses, said, "Small rooms or dwellings set the mind in the right path; large ones cause it to go astray." Some two thousand years before da Vinci, the Talmud said, "If you grasp a small amount, you will have it. If you grasp too much, you will have nothing."

Our eyes are often bigger than our stomach, and we take much more than we can possibly digest. On the other hand, we think something to be so enormous that we consider it impossible to conquer. Either way, nothing gets accomplished.

The only proper approach to reality is to take bite-size portions. Then we do not take more than we can handle, nor are we frightened away from attempting to achieve.

Sobriety is just one of many challenges to be taken in bite-size pieces. The proper amount for the average individual, regardless of the challenge, is "one day at a time."

Think Before You Make Your Move
❧

"Grant me the serenity to accept that which I cannot change."

How often do we wish that more situations were changeable! While many factors are totally beyond our capacity to change, there are things we can do to avoid situations becoming unchangeable.

A rabbi who had difficulty impressing a person with the gravity of his behavior invited him to a game of chess. On several occasions the rabbi asked to retract a move, and the opponent granted the request. Finally, the latter's patience was exhausted. "You can't keep doing that, Rabbi," he said. "Once you have taken your hand off the piece, the move is completed. It is final and irrevocable."

"Exactly the point I have been trying to make with you, my friend," the rabbi said. "If a move in a mere game is irrevocable, how much more so are moves in life. Many of our actions are final, and we must give at least as much forethought to our actions in life and their consequences as to our moves in chess."

If what we are about to do may become unchangeable, how much thought have we given it before doing it?

Do We Know Our Destination?
❦

We cannot know where we *are* unless we know where we *should be.*

The first recorded dialogue between God and man, as recorded in the Bible, begins with God asking man, "Where are you?"—Genesis 3:9. This question is one God continues to ask us, and one we should continue to ask ourselves each day.

However, this question is virtually meaningless without a reference point. Otherwise, the answer is simply "I'm in St. Louis." The question has meaning only if we have a goal in life. Then it means "Are you a bit closer to the goal than yesterday, or farther away?" Or perhaps "Are you on the path altogether?"

Most people are far from stupid. We will not accept a goal in life that is an insult to our dignity. The problem is not that we may have chosen the wrong goal, but that too often we have given no thought to *any* goal. We are swept up in the business of living, overwhelmed by the commercialism that preys on our weakness to live more comfortably, that we only consider the *how* of life, and not the *why.*

In addiction we had the wrong answer to *How?* In all likelihood, the question *Why?* had never even arisen.

Solitude or Fellowship?
🍏

Recovery meetings have an intrinsic value.

Many things occur at meetings: we share personal experiences in addiction and recovery, we discuss the Steps and pertinent issues in recovery, we find a sponsor, we exchange phone numbers, and we broaden contacts with sober people. But over and above these, the meetings have a value by virtue of their being a gathering of people.

Why do all faiths encourage communal prayer? Isn't individual prayer just as good? Will any believer deny that God listens to each person's prayer even if it is offered in solitude rather than with others in a chapel?

Religious leaders have always known that there is strength in group activity. When people pray together they reinforce one another's belief. The quality of prayer is different when it is communal.

This holds true for meetings as well, especially in a recovery fellowship where interdependence is felt so keenly. A guest speaker from another city said, "There is nothing I *could* do without you, and there is nothing I *cannot* do when I have you." Although he was speaking to a group of total strangers, he was nevertheless sincere in his statement, because the *you* is the fellowship everywhere—an incomparable source of strength.

We share this strength at meetings.

Flattery Can Be Dangerous

🍂

Insincere flattery is unbecoming, but when we praise someone who behaves improperly, it is frankly dangerous.

When someone who does wrong receives praise instead of rebuke, it reinforces that behavior. Whatever rationalizations the person may have to justify that behavior are supported further, and the person loses any chance of recognizing the impropriety.

When others see a wrong-doer receiving praise, it diminishes their incentive for just behavior. Why should they deprive themselves of things that can be obtained illicitly when dishonest behavior is rewarded? Furthermore, even if a person knows we are fawning, his attitudes nevertheless are affected, eventually believing his own lies.

"Smooth talk makes for a slippery course"—Proverbs 26:28. People who fawn are likely to be disillusioned on discovering that their insincere praise does not bring the result anticipated. We are then doubly disappointed: to have compromised our integrity and to have received nothing in return.

"Rigorous honesty" is an essential component of recovery, and is most beneficial in the long run.

When in Doubt, Listen

Take the cotton out of your ears and put it in your mouth.

This advice applies to the nonaddict as well as the recovering person. The Talmud says, "All my years I grew up among the wise, and I found nothing more beneficial than silence"—Ethics of the Fathers 1:17.

The philosopher Aristotle taught that virtue lies somewhere between two extremes—courage lies between recklessness and cowardice, thrift between miserliness and extravagance. But virtue is not necessarily midway between two poles and may be closer to one extreme.

Absolute silence is not virtuous, because refraining from saying the proper thing can be wrong. But virtuous speech is much closer to the extreme of silence than to that of babbling. We regret things we have said much more than the things we did not say.

Furthermore, when we are talking we cannot listen. We hardly learn anything by talking, but we can learn much by listening. Silence may indeed be most beneficial.

Marriage Can Flourish in Recovery

A recovering marriage can thrive.

While addiction can inflict much suffering on a family—sometimes so much that it cannot be forgotten even with the finest recovery—many marriages not only survive but even thrive in recovery.

The principle for a harmonious recovering marriage is no different from that for a nonaddiction relationship: respect for the partner's individuality and his or her right to be different. Compatibility does not require similarity. Rather, it requires respect of difference. Some of the most idyllic relationships are between two unlike people.

During addiction there is no mutual respect. The addict's self-will-run-riot does not tolerate dissenting opinion, while the spouse can see only wrong in the addict's ideas. Recovery requires new ground rules. As we develop humility, we can respect the other's opinions. Tolerance of difference permits intimacy and love to grow. And an awareness of the dangers of intolerance, as appreciated in recovery, can result in a most compatible relationship.

Consider the Future

The key to recovery is consideration of the future.

There are several legends about an elderly person who planted a tree. When asked if he really thought he would live long enough to eat of its fruit, he replied, "Of course not. I am planting this tree for my children and grandchildren."

We all leave our belongings to future generations, but we gather them primarily for ourselves. The person who plants the tree, however, knows that he will never benefit from its fruit. His work is totally for the future.

A recovering person in his sixties began buying savings bonds for his new grandchild as his wedding gift to her, a wedding he knew he was unlikely to attend. He had turned the corner to sobriety.

In active addiction there is no consideration for the future. Our future is grossly sacrificed in favor of momentary gratification. Rather than mere abstinence, one of the signs of sobriety is beginning to do things for the future—for our children or community.

Turning Destructive Energy into a Positive Force

In recovery we transform negatives into positives.

In the fairy tale "Rumpelstiltskin," straw is spun into gold; the greater the supply of straw, the more gold is produced.

In recovery, many negative traits are converted into positives. Just as no prospector goes looking for straw to turn into gold, neither does any rational person develop negative traits in order to transform them into positives. However, if they happen to be there, the net result in recovery can be a wealth of character assets.

The energy, cunning, and determination that were perfected in addiction can be powerful forces for good when properly channeled. When I commented to some recovering people on how they were extending themselves to an extraordinary degree to assist others in early recovery, they replied, "I'll only go as far to help somebody as I would have gone for a drink or a fix, and that's a helluva long way."

Nothing stands in the way of an addict who wants a chemical. When this determination is applied to positive goals, no obstacle is too great.

There is No Logic to Addiction

Logic has little effect on addiction.

A young woman who was in coma for two weeks following drug use, and who spent a month in intensive care, narrowly escaping death, requested admission to a treatment center. "I know I need help," she said. "This may sound crazy, but although I know I was on the verge of death and that I have serious heart disease, there is this thought in my head that I can still use again."

This is a person who very much wishes to live, who has no doubt that drugs are lethal, and yet she has an irrational drive to use again. She is not consciously suicidal, but we can compare her drive to that of lemmings who seek their own death.

In the Biblical account of Adam and Eve in the Garden of Eden, God tells man, "If you eat of this fruit, you shall surely die." The serpent says, "Do not worry. You will not die if you eat." The Biblical story thus teaches us that temptation can blind a person to inevitable consequences.

Adam and Eve succumbed. But being the only two humans in the world, they had no support program to help them. The young woman above is fortunate because she can enlist the help of countless people in recovery. Recovering people say, "Don't analyze. Utilize!" What they mean is, "Don't try applying logic. Use what works."

326

The Bigger the Boast, the Smaller the Self-Esteem

If we know we are great, we do not have to prove it.

Little children climb onto a chair or table and announce, "See how big I am! I can almost touch the ceiling." Or they put on their parents' clothes to make believe that they are grown-ups.

All that changes when we grow up is that we do not stand on chairs to demonstrate our height. The underlying pattern is unchanged, however. In whatever way we feel small, we try to show that we are big.

We see people who are name-droppers, or who otherwise try to impress people with their importance. We think, "What a huge, inflated ego that person has." Actually, that person feels terribly depleted and acts in desperation to convince others of his or her importance. This person wants to have a feeling of self-worth, hoping to hear the equivalent of "Look how big Johnny is" when the child stands high on the chair.

Instead of being annoyed with the pomp and arrogance of the person who behaves egotistically, can we not find enough compassion to feel for someone who feels so unworthy that he or she takes such desperate measures?

God Understands Our Pain

We can relate to God *as He understands us*.

While we must learn to accept unpleasant things with serenity, this does not preclude feeling angry when we feel treated unfairly by God.

During severe suffering, it is unrealistic to be serene. When pain is intense, we have only one desire: to be relieved of the pain. Since God is all powerful and can relieve the pain, we are angry with Him for not doing so and for allowing the suffering. This anger at God is not blasphemous.

Once the pain has disappeared, our faith in God should allow us to be serene again and accept our experience. We are not expected to accept the suffering of the moment, but we are expected to accept the pain of the past.

The anger we have at the time of the pain need not be considered sinful, because we can relate to God *as He understands us*. He has total knowledge of our emotional makeup, and expects us to react normally. The average person's faith cannot override an intense pain experience. But when the pain is a matter of history, faith should become operative, and serenity will prevail.

Giving Thanks

Since this is the week of Thanksgiving, it is appropriate to share a card that I received from a woman who had completed her first year of recovery.

"I can't help but remember the past Thanksgiving holidays and how I hated them. I felt that I had absolutely nothing to be thankful for, and unfortunately, I made that known to all those around me. I know that this attitude caused my family and friends to dread what should have been a pleasant holiday.

"This year, I wish to say that this Thanksgiving is special—I am sober and clean—and I am thankful. I have been given a second chance! I can now partake of life. I can smile sincerely and cry occasionally and even feel a little love and peace at times.

"I am grateful for God's hand leading me to help, and I am grateful to all those who shared their experiences, strength, hope, and courage, which enabled me to start in a new life.

"I have been able to continue at college for my final year, after catching up on the course work last year. I invite everyone to join this Thanksgiving celebration with me."

Gratitude can be an exhilarating feeling, but too often we take things for granted, and our gratitude consists of little more than words. When someone who is experiencing sincere gratitude shares it with us, we are drawn into sharing the freshness of the feeling. Let us all join this young woman in sharing a sincere Thanksgiving.

Humility Is Essential
❦

Gratitude and humility go together.

For many people, Thanksgiving Day is the only time they focus on gratitude. Some people have difficulty in feeling grateful and especially in expressing gratitude.

As a rule, people in recovery do not have much difficulty with this. They express their gratitude for their sobriety, for having been given a second chance, for the recovery of their loved ones and the salvation of their families, and for the support of the fellowship. But why is it easier for people in recovery to express gratitude?

Some people have difficulty with gratitude because, if they acknowledge a kindness they will feel obligated. Others feel that acknowledging a favor is admitting dependence; their ego stands in the way of saying, "Thank you for doing something for me." Indeed, some people go so far as to feel resentment toward anyone who has done anything for them.

Recovery requires humility. Active addiction is often characterized as an ego gone wild. So recovery requires not only abstinence but also elimination of character defects, one of which is an inflated ego. Humility is essential for recovery.

This is why there are frequent expressions of thankfulness at Twelve Step meetings. People whose egos stand in the way of expressing gratitude are not too likely to be at these meetings, because their inflated ego has not let them admit their powerlessness.

Giving Thanks for Sobriety

"If anyone would have told me that I would be grateful for the intervention done on me, I would have said they were mad. I was living in a beautiful home with my two cats. Yes, I took a few drinks at night, one or two sleeping pills, and an occasional Valium. I was not bothering anyone. What right did anyone have to interfere with my life?

"I did not realize that I could not fully enjoy my grandchildren whom I loved. But for some reason, my daughters never asked me to babysit.

"Today alcohol and pills are no longer my companions. I babysit for my grandchildren, and when my daughters leave for vacation, they entrust their children to me. I love them, and I love the feeling that I can be trusted. I am grateful for sobriety."

Only We Can Develop Will Power
❦

In our age of transplant surgery, recovery should be simple.

If kidney failure threatens our life, a successful kidney transplant will allow us to live a normal life. Likewise, all we need to recover from chemical addiction is realize that our will can be affected by a mysterious disease, and a "will transplant" can be life saving.

Does the will become diseased? A bright medical resident at the top of his class said, "I knew that continued use of drugs could ruin my career and destroy me and my family's future. When I got the urge to use I would take out the picture of my wife and baby and say, 'You won't do this to them.' Sometimes I would cry over the picture for fifteen minutes, then shoot up." If that is not a disease of the will, what is?

We look for a "will donor." But in this case, family members are not satisfactory; it is not wise to substitute a spouse's or parent's will for our own. It is much wiser to take the will of a Higher Power, whether it be a deity or a group of recovering people whose collective will is functional.

Accepting a kidney transplant is not ego deflating; neither should be a "will transplant."

An Unhealthy Escape

Escaping from ourselves is destructive.

A business executive who rejected help with his drinking problem said, "I know exactly what to do. I never drink at the office, so I will take work home and keep myself busy."

In the absence of work to distract him, this man resorted to alcohol. Although he was not planning to substitute another chemical for alcohol, his escape into work was nevertheless unhealthy. It would ultimately either fail or result in a stress-related disease. We cannot escape from ourselves over the long haul, nor should we need to do so.

When this man's workaholism failed, he returned to the alcohol escapism and eventually entered the recovery program. Since doing so, he has begun to enjoy vacations with his family. He can now spend time fishing. He can be alone with himself because he is comfortable with the self that he discovered to be likeable after all.

Various addictions can be escapes, but there are escapes of other kinds as well. Escaping from a burning building is proper, but escaping from ourselves is not. A frank analysis of our personality and correction of character defects allow us to appreciate ourselves. This is accomplished by working Steps Four to Ten.

Some Tolerance Can Be Deadly
🍎

Addiction is characterized by tolerance.

Tolerance is an adaptive mechanism, whereby we no longer feel the effect of a particular dose of chemical and progressively increase the dose taken. Our body becomes tolerant of increasing doses, and allows us to continue to function until the effects of the chemical ultimately result in dysfunction.

Codependence often mimics addiction. The family puts up with a given dose of addictive behavior and develops a tolerance, so that it remains functional while the dose of sick behavior continues to increase until a rock-bottom event brings the family to its senses. Ironically, the addict is at somewhat of an advantage, because healthy family members can intervene, whereas intervention is much more difficult with a codependent family.

The recovery process for the family is similar to that for the addict, beginning with surrender, accepting powerlessness over the life of the addict, and going through an inventory and making amends. The family may be unaware of how many people, both within and outside the family, may have been harmed by the codependent behavior. Finally, just as the addict must find a goal in life other than use of the chemical, the family must find a goal other than accommodating the addict.

Recognizing Distortion
🍂

We must climb only over obstacles that really exist.

People adjusting to bifocals report that initially they may fall when ascending or descending stairs. When they get to the top or bottom step, they see a step that isn't there, and when they raise or lower their feet to traverse it, they stumble. Likewise, we can fall by trying to overcome an obstacle that is not there as well as by seeing one that is there.

Many obstacles exist in our mind rather than in reality, but when we deal with them as though they were real, we stumble. We may defensively approach someone who is not an aggressor, or overreact to trivia as though they were catastrophes. An innocent remark can be perceived as an insult, and our angry reply can convert a friend into an enemy.

Whereas we readily recognize the distortions of perception that occur with bifocals, we have little insight into the distortions of communications. A simple inquiry, "What did you mean by that?" can clarify a comment. Or we can ask objective observers for their interpretation.

We need all our energy to deal with the real difficulties in life. We can ill afford to squander our strength on nonexisting obstacles, which only drain our limited resources and create new difficulties.

335

We Are Never Alone

We need never feel alone.

Ever since we were children, abandonment has been a source of anxiety. Some of us can recall the terror of being alone, while others manage to repress it. Psychologists state that, in the latter case, repressed feelings continue to affect our emotions and influence our behavior. They also say that the fear of death is nothing other than this terrible fear of abandonment.

A theologian who experienced a severe depression wrote that in his darkest moments, when he felt so terribly alone, he was comforted by the verse of the Psalms: "If I rise to the heavens, You are there, and if I descend into the depths, You are there too"—Psalms 139:8. "I may indeed be in the depths of hell," he said, "but God was there with me, and I was not alone." People who have recovered from a near-death experience describe the feeling of being in the presence of God. Again the words of the Psalmist give one courage: "Though I walk through the valley of the shadow of death, You are with me"—Psalm 23:4.

While God is always with us, it is even more comforting when we can think, "I have always been with Him, so why should He not be with me now?"

We can live a life that banishes the terror of abandonment forever.

Growth Through Adversity
🍎

Overcoming hurdles strengthens our character.

A young professional woman with several years of sobriety was treated very shabbily in her application for a position because of her history of addiction. She stated, "I really don't have any resentments against this person who was so unfair, because he did me a great favor. I've survived this ordeal, and the next one I encounter will be just a piece of pie."

Adversities are not pleasant, but life is full of them. We cannot escape them, and we need strength to cope effectively.

Children raised in a sterile environment may have rosy cheeks and appear robust and healthy, but their first contact with bacteria will be lethal. Our body produces antibodies and other substances to fight off infections only as a result of being exposed to germs, which is essentially why immunization works. To protect children from all disease-causing organisms may appear to be a kindness, but it leaves them totally defenseless in the real world.

We need not love people who have mistreated us, but surviving one ordeal strengthens us and prepares us for the difficulties that are inevitable in life.

It's More Than Just Self-Help

❦

In helping others, we help ourselves.

Tom is a prominent attorney who reluctantly admitted his alcoholism. His attendance at AA was infrequent and perfunctory. He would usually remain in the corridor for fear that someone in the meeting room might recognize him.

One time when he was pacing the corridor a young man came in and asked, "Are you with AA?"

"Yes," Tom answered.

"Can you help me?" the young man asked. "I just got out of detox and they told me to go to an AA meeting and get a sponsor." The young man appeared so needy and pathetic that Tom offered to sponsor him.

Then it occurred to Tom, "What have I done? I don't know anything about this program. How can I help this poor kid?" Tom then decided to get to know what AA is all about in order to help the young man.

When I called Tom to congratulate him on his fifteenth anniversary of sobriety, he said, "I am dry fifteen years, but sober only twelve. It wasn't until I entered AA that I became sober, and I owe it all to that kid."

Try helping someone. It works.

No One Is Turned Away

❦

Recovering people are wealthier than the wealthy.

Some wealthy people have summer or winter homes in exotic places. But few have a home in every country in the world.

Someone defined *home* as "a place from which you can't get turned away." AA and NA meeting rooms, then, are homes because no addict is ever turned away. Since there are fellowship meetings in virtually every country on earth, recovering people have homes everywhere. The only rich people who can make this claim are those who are in the fellowship.

A man visited Spain on business. He had been told that missing meetings was risky for relapse. Wishing to maintain his precious sobriety but not able to locate an English-speaking meeting, he attended a Spanish meeting. "I was welcomed by everyone with handshakes and hugs. I sat through the entire meeting without understanding a single word that was spoken, but it was okay because I knew exactly what they were saying."

Not only do recovering people have homes and friends all over the world, but they also can understand more languages than the most prolific linguist—as long as the subject being discussed is recovery from addiction.

The Difference Between Self-Knowledge and Self-Absorption

Knowledge of oneself is important; preoccupation with oneself can be harmful.

We have emphasized self-awareness and self-esteem. While it is important to have a correct concept of ourselves, it is equally important that we do not become so preoccupied with ourselves that everyone else is eliminated from consideration.

Preoccupation with ourselves can become an obsession, in which our personal desires are all that matter. Clearly this is not intended in recovery from addiction. To the contrary, the addictive attitude is, "I've got to have what I want when I want it, and the rest of the world be damned." Elimination of character defects, making amends, and attainment of humility in recovery are the antithesis of self-centeredness.

A recovering person said, "I looked in myself so hard that I lost sight of everyone else." Unless we are cautious, this can happen in abstinence as well as in addiction, and we then have "dry drunk" syndrome.

Participation in the program, sharing with others, and helping others in sobriety help prevent this obsession with ourselves. This is another reason why meetings are important. Solitary recovery runs the risk of self-centered abstinence.

Finding the Right Approach
❧

We must have serenity in order to be courageous.

There is a phenomenon known as the "William Tell" syndrome, based on the story of the famous archer ordered to shoot an apple perched on his son's head. The average person instructed to shoot at a target would hold the bow and arrow steady, and if lucky might hit the bull's-eye. If it were missed, it would not be a catastrophe. If, however, he were ordered to shoot at an apple on his son's head, the dread of what would happen if he missed is so terrifying that he would tremble and could not possibly hold the bow steady. His attempt would be doomed to fail because of anxiety.

If we approach a challenge with serenity, we can see things in proper perspective, come to a correct decision, and act constructively. If we approach the same challenge with intense anxiety, our perception, thought, and action are all distorted, and we are virtually certain to fail.

When we share a problem with others, we elucidate it for ourselves. Sometimes we benefit from the wisdom and experience of others with a solution. At the very least, describing the problem to others can help us discover factors of which we had been unaware. With the proper perspective, we can find the courage to act.

Building Character
❦

Character growth is intrinsically progressive.

Character is composed of several elements, and much like the decor of a room, they must be compatible. Just as gross conflicts in style and color in furnishings are not well tolerated, so we do not tolerate gross incompatibility in character traits.

Greed, envy, selfishness, inconsideration, lying, arrogance, and vanity are mutually compatible. Kindness, truth, self-sacrifice, humility, consideration, and benevolence are mutually compatible. But any element in the first group is incompatible with any element in the second group.

Active addiction is characterized by traits of the first group. As we begin sobriety, correction of character defects and replacement by virtuous character traits makes all other defects incompatible. If we maintain sobriety, the movement can be in only one direction—making all character traits compatible with a virtuous one. Thus, whatever the beginning may be, the result is the same: all character defects are eventually eliminated, replaced by positive traits.

We need only to make a beginning, and the rest will follow.

May I Never Forget

Sometimes we do not appreciate the positive until we look at the negative.

At some meetings, the Twelve Promises or Rewards of sobriety are recited: freedom instead of addictive enslavement; serenity instead of anxiety; usefulness instead of uselessness; love of people instead of fear of people; pride instead of self-pity; and so on.

While these are certainly important incentives, they are not as impressive as an awareness of what happens if we return to chemical use. All we need do is reverse the reading of the rewards: addictive enslavement instead of freedom; anxiety instead of serenity; uselessness instead of usefulness; fear of people instead of love of people.

A recovering person said, "The worst day in sobriety is far better than the best day in addiction." The problem is that addictive thinking is very cunning, and the same mechanism that operates to produce denial during active addiction can produce impaired memory in recovery. We may forget the horror of active addiction.

An advantage in helping newcomers in recovery is that we are reminded of the many distresses addiction produces. While people prefer to put unpleasant experiences out of their mind, it is not uncommon to hear people in recovery pray, "May I never forget." It is helpful to remember the hell we wish to never re-enter.

Straight Talk
❧

Honesty should be good enough; why does the recovery program insist on "rigorous" honesty?

The two terms are identical, and the only reason the word *rigorous* is added is to emphasize that honesty is either rigorous or it is not honesty at all. "Almost true" is a lie.

There is no difficulty thinking up rationalizations for little white lies. It is common to beat around the bush and not state clearly what we want or what we feel.

People who are not recovering from addiction or codependency may be able to get by with this kind of honesty, which is not really cheating anyone. The lies are essentially to ourselves. From an ethical viewpoint, we are avoiding harm to others, so this type of honesty might be condoned.

But this does not hold true for people in recovery. A violation of self-honesty is at the root of much addictive or codependent behavior. Unless we become "rigorously honest," eliminating all half-truths, recovery is incomplete.

Straight talk is simple. Dishonesty is complex. Recovery requires keeping it simple, which means being rigorously honest.

We Create Our Own Punishment
❦

The program refers to "God as we *understand* Him"; many people have a concept of "God as we *misunderstand* Him."

Parental discipline invariably involves reward and punishment. This has been so since time immemorial, and perhaps cannot be otherwise. In the process of teaching children about God, it is either explicitly stated or implied that God operates the way parents do. We grow up thinking that God wields a huge club, waiting to pounce on us if we misbehave.

A more careful reading of religious writings indicates a different concept. The biblical phrase, "It is the evil that destroys the wicked" means that the punishment for a wrong deed lies in the act itself. Improper behavior contains its own painful consequences, some of which follow immediately and others only after some delay.

In addiction we learn that no one need punish us for abusing chemicals. Chemicals carry more painful consequences than anyone could think of. When we recover, we can apply this valuable lesson to everything else in life. We understand that it is not God who punishes us, but that we precipitate our own punishment when we behave improperly.

Recovery allows us to dispense with our juvenile *misunderstanding* of God.

People-Pleasing

Recovery from addiction involves more than just stopping use of chemicals.

As one person stated, "The problem isn't the alcohol, it's alcoho*lism*, and when you take away the alcohol, you still have the *ism* to deal with."

One of the more common components of the *ism* is "people-pleasing," or the inability to say no when that is what we really want to say, but we are afraid to refuse because the person might not like us anymore. What it really comes down to is that we are buying friendship.

During active addiction we become angry with ourselves for not taking a firm stand on our own behalf and for letting others take advantage of us; we also develop resentments toward others. It's almost a sure thing that this combination of anger and resentment toward others will result in chemical use.

Why should we have to buy friendship? Perhaps because we don't think it can be had free. Maybe if we thought better of ourselves and felt we were likable, we wouldn't *need* to buy friendship.

People will like us even if we are sometimes unable to comply with their requests. If we have an erroneous picture of ourselves, we may think that we are unlikable, and people-pleasing is just one of the many consequences of this negativity. Sobriety can help us develop the self-awareness that allows us to better appreciate ourselves, and to know that others do also.

True Happiness Requires a Lifetime Commitment

The writer Samuel Johnson said, "Great works are performed not by strength but by perseverance."

Perseverance is a rather unpopular concept in the modern world. Science has provided us with technologies that have greater capacity than whatever was available heretofore. Computers can solve mathematical problems in fractions of a second. Fax machines and overnight mail can deliver messages that used to require Pony Express. But I am not yet aware of a computer that can be fed words or musical notes to be rapidly combined to result in the equivalent of a Beethoven symphony, a Dostoyevsky novel, or a Shakespearian drama. As far as masterpieces are concerned, Samuel Johnson is still correct.

What about our lives? What about happiness? What about self-fulfillment? Are these comparable to technological miracles, or are they more akin to the artistic masterpieces? Can a machine produce them or do they require perseverance?

Addicts have tried to achieve happiness with alcohol, heroin, or cocaine, and self-fulfillment with marijuana or LSD. The consensus is that these do not work, and that human goals belong with the great works that require perseverance.

Perhaps people need to consider their lives to be great works.

A Life Without Goals is an Empty Chaos

A path of life that is merely self-gratifying is not a path at all.

Particles of matter that have energy and move about in a closed space display chaotic motion. They bounce off the walls of the container or off each other, and there is no pattern to their movement. They are not going from one place to another. They have no goal, hence they have no path, because a path is nothing but a way to reach some goal.

If we seek only self-gratification, we are essentially living a chaotic life, attracted by whatever is available and repelled by obstacles. We are not following a path.

This often happens in addiction because the chemical dictates where we go. People who have a goal or follow a path in life cannot relate to the chaotic movement of the addict. Children of addicts who should have been guided in a path of life may never have observed this consistency. Even if they grow up to be nonusers, they may lack the skills to choose and follow a path. Even without chemicals, their behavior is random and their lives chaotic.

"He guides me in straight paths"—Psalms 23:3. A straight path is by far preferable, but even a winding path can lead somewhere. It is having no path that is intolerable.

Our Egos Can Get in the Way
❦

Humility depends on just being human.

A physician who specializes in the treatment of addiction states that he must avoid meetings attended by his patients because, "They ask me questions, and while I don't mind answering them, I become a doctor instead of just a person. I am at that meeting because I need help as a person, and when I function as an authoritative doctor, my ego gets in the way of my recovery."

This is a valuable insight. Recovery works for *people*, not for doctors or lawyers or professors or executives. When people shed their professional identity and are just human beings, the ego moves out of the way, and humility, the necessary ingredient for recovery, appears.

We do not need a title to have an ego. Anyone can develop an ego out of thin air. Sometimes the latter egos are more difficult to dismantle than those having some substance.

When we realize that addiction is an equal opportunity destroyer and can affect us equally, then we share our humanity with other people and can achieve humility. We allow ourselves to be helped.

Real Growth Takes Time and Effort
🍂

We should learn to appreciate growth that occurs in latency.

A recovering woman stated on her fourth anniversary, "It has taken me four years to finally feel good about myself." Although it was not until after four years that she became aware she was a good person, it is absurd to think that nothing had occurred during that time and that everything blossomed overnight.

We may not see the chick until it breaks out of a shell, but it was certainly growing and developing for a long time before it emerged. Similarly, we may not see or feel progress in our personality development until a certain point, but it is certainly happening.

"The only thing I did right was not drink and go to meetings," the woman said. Fortunately, she had the trust that if she followed instructions, the desired results would eventually be forthcoming. Admittedly, four years is a long time, and a great deal of patience is required, but the reassurance of people who have been there can make the waiting period tolerable.

We can be assured that latency is very much a time of growth, but one where the growth is beneath the surface. As long as we abstain from chemicals and work the Steps, real growth is constantly occurring.

You Cannot Control the Future
❦

Too much concentration on the future generates anxiety.

We must plan realistically for the future, but remember that the future remains unpredictable. There are simply no guarantees. Trying to cover every possible eventuality will exhaust our energies and ultimately result in disappointment, because there is just no way that all possibilities can be covered.

The wise Solomon said, "I therefore observed that there is nothing better for man than to be happy in what he is doing. For who can enable him to see what will be after him?"—Ecclesiastes 3:22.

Interest rates fluctuate, the stock market zig-zags, mighty corporations go under while small businesses blossom. If we act reasonably and realize our limitations, we can at least enjoy the present. If we become preoccupied with assuring ourselves of the future, we enjoy neither.

This is especially important in recovery, where we must shed the delusion of control. Although we may realize that there is no control over chemicals, we may retain the delusion that we can control our economic future. This is why we must decide at what point it is appropriate to "Let go and let God." If we are unable to make this determination, we can ask for help to do so.

You are a Beautiful Person

Thinking positively about ourselves is not always an easy task.

What could be more pleasant than having a positive self-concept? Yet some people have great difficulty with this.

To emphasize the importance of a positive self-concept, I instructed all members of a group accustomed to identifying themselves as "My name is John Doe, and I am an alcoholic or addict" to instead say, "My name is John Doe. *I am a beautiful person*, with the disease of alcoholism or drug addiction." One young woman in the group was unable to say the phrase, "I am a beautiful person."

Since addiction is a disease, an addict is really a *person with a disease*. It is the disease that has given rise to most character defects. The disease is something superimposed upon us—it is not the person within us. The inability to say, "I am a beautiful person with the disease" may betray a lack of conviction in the disease concept of addiction, and a moralistic attitude that an addict is a bad person.

It is important to recognize addiction as a disease, and that when we are free of the disease, our inherent goodness will be revealed. Knowing that in recovery we will be worthy, deserving, and lovable gives us the strength and courage to recover.

Don't Use Others as an Excuse

We should not measure ourselves by others.

A recovering physician stated that he worked at an addiction treatment center. Rather than this giving him greater insight into his addiction, it reinforced his denial because his clients were so much more advanced in their addiction than he was. In comparison, he did not think he was abusing chemicals.

This is a particularly treacherous form of addiction. A recovering person said, "If you're going to have a problem with alcohol, my suggestion is to drink heavily when you're young, get into a great deal of trouble, and get it over with. My problem was that I never got into any trouble, and I slowly pickled my brain for thirty years."

If we measured ourselves by what we could be, we might discover that we are performing far below our optimum. But since we may not be able to see this, it is wise to keep our ears open and be receptive to critical observations from others. In fact, we are wise to invite critique, since even early addictive chemical use can make us oblivious to our relative dysfunction.

One woman said, "Maybe I wasn't as sick as others, but I was as sick as I wanted to be." That is a constructive observation.

How We Become What We Despise

"Only a power greater than myself could restore me to sanity."

We frequently hear, "I was absolutely repulsed by my father's or mother's drinking. I hated him or her for it. I swore that I would never become like that." Or the doctor or nurse who says, "They would bring drunks into the emergency room who were shabby and deteriorated, and would go into the DTs. I swore that would never happen to me." Yet these people relate how they went on to become what had been so abhorrent to them.

An alcoholic physician developed alcoholic liver disease. As soon as his daily blood test showed that liver function had been restored, he immediately began drinking, leading to a recurrence of the liver disease, which he knew would occur.

Psychologists suggest many theories for this: identification with the aggressor; a challenge to drink or use to prove that we are invincible; an unconscious death wish, and so on. Whatever the specific dynamics, one thing is for certain: such behavior is insanity.

If we know we have the potential for insanity, and we wish to avoid the disastrous consequences of this insanity, we designate some friends to be on the alert: "Tell me if you see me doing anything crazy." This is one of the things that transpires in the recovery fellowship, where a sponsor or friends can look for any signs of irrationality, and thereby prevent self-destructive behavior.

Let the Miracle of Sobriety Occur
❦

Sobriety may sometimes come from a breakthrough.

A new volcano makes its appearance when molten lava that has been stored in the earth's core slowly makes its way through the earth's crust, erupting with great force. For thousands of years this lava had been deep below anyone's reach or awareness.

People have within them a core of dignity and self-respect, but in some people this core is buried deep, covered by various happenings in life. Without a sense of dignity, we may behave in a way that is unbecoming. Without an awareness of our dignity, we have no idea it exists. Unfortunately, undignified behavior continues to add layers of concealment, in a self-reinforcing, destructive, vicious cycle.

Like the lava that slowly works its way to the earth's surface, the dignity that lies at the core of a human being pushes its way up until one day it breaks through the surface. Out of nowhere, we feel "I am too good for this. I have no right to be anything less than I can be." Without external pressure or coercion, the miracle of sobriety can then occur.

The Danger of Seeking Scapegoats
❧

Scapegoating should be avoided.

Both the addict and codependents scapegoat, sometimes using each other and sometimes an outside party.

People who have grown up in a dysfunctional home have legitimate reasons for their emotional problems, yet finding fault with our parents does nothing to resolve these problems. The purpose of self-help groups and treatment for children of addicted parents is not to place blame, but to learn effective coping techniques, and to find ways to eliminate whatever character defects or emotional hang-ups may have resulted.

Some people misinterpret this concept and look for scapegoats. They may even create dysfunction where none existed. A cartoon shows an immense arena where a convention of "Children of *Normal* Parents" is being held, with one person sitting among thousands of empty seats. Granted, there are many dysfunctional families, but not all families are dysfunctional—unless you have a reason to wish to see them this way.

Refusal to recognize your background as dysfunctional may obstruct recovery. On the other hand, scapegoating your parents as responsible for all your problems in order to justify your behavior instead of modifying it is equally unhealthy.

Inflexible Opinions Can Drive People Away
❦

Other people have as much right to their opinions as we have to our own.

The place of dogma in religion is arguable, but justifiable. To someone who believes in God, He is omniscient and perfect, hence cannot make mistakes nor change His mind as a result of newly acquired information. Since humans are neither omniscient nor perfect, we should be amenable to modifying the way we think. Since we are not always right, others may be right.

Henry Ford is alleged to have said, "People can have any color car they want as long as it is black." Of course, as long as he was the sole manufacturer of the car, he could control what everyone got, even if he could not control what they want. In absence of such exclusiveness, obstinate insistence on getting our own way will simply drive customers to competitors, much to our detriment.

This is as true in human relationships as it is in industry. Insistence on our own opinion will drive people toward others who are more accommodating, and the resulting isolation and loneliness will be far more costly than the loss of customers.

We need not change colors like a chameleon, but neither should we be rigid and inflexible in our opinions.

Beware of the Mind's Distortions
🍏

The human mind is ingenious, but can be deceptive.

We are sound asleep and we dream of an ice-cream vendor's wagon, whose bells are clanging. After a few moments we are aroused, and we realize that the ringing we heard in the dream was in reality the alarm clock, and that our minds had concocted a dream in which the bell would fit into the scene. This was the mind's effort to disguise the sound of the bell so that our pleasant sleep would not be disturbed.

The entire scene in the dream, of which the bell was so logical a part, was all planned, staged, and produced within a fraction of a millisecond at the very first sound of the alarm. That is the incomparable lightning efficiency of our mind when it tries to protect us from disturbance, even at the cost of distorting reality.

It is absurd to think that this occurs only in sleep. To the contrary, the mind is probably more efficient when awake. How often, then, may we be rendered oblivious to reality by our mind trying to protect our peace at all costs? If the dream succeeds in making us unaware of the alarm clock, we oversleep and miss important events. If our waking minds succeed in making us oblivious to reality, it may be even more to our detriment.

Touching base with others and having an open mind to their observations can help us avoid the pitfalls of good intentions by our greatest of all "enablers"—our own mind.

Envy Makes Us Ugly

Few feelings are as sick as envy.

Envy is a character trait soundly condemned in all ethical writings, from the Ten Commandments through all psychology and philosophy books. However, the extent of its pathology did not strike me until recently.

A gentleman drove me to a meeting, and was having great difficulty finding a parking space. One vacant space was designated for the handicapped. As we were sharing our frustration at being late for the meeting, a car with a handicap license plate parked in the vacant space, whereupon my companion remarked, "Lucky son-of-a-gun!"

Lucky? Is it advantageous to be deprived of the freedom to ambulate easily? Would that handicapped person not have preferred to park four blocks away if only he were able to walk that distance?

Of course, we sometimes envy people who have more money or other things that we may value, but in the final analysis, to want what someone else has must be an intense and irrational emotion if it causes us to be envious of a handicapped person. Emotions that can be as bizarre as that are best gotten rid of.

Sober Celebration

A newly recovering physician expressed his frustration. "I'm angry," he said, "because everywhere around me people are drinking and having a good time, and I don't dare take a drink." A doctor who was in his fifth year of sobriety responded, "When I found out that I couldn't drink anymore, it was a sense of relief. I don't have to fight that battle anymore."

It's pretty much how you look at it. You can resent it, or you can breathe a sigh of relief. Just think how much energy you can save, how your mind can be free of worry. There's no need to try to control the uncontrollable anymore, or to cover up, or to manufacture excuses and face disappointments.

One woman refused to enter treatment unless she could have a leave of absence to be with her family on Christmas. I told her she could have this on one condition: that she tell me anything that transpired in the past two Christmases she spent with her family. She could not remember a single thing, because she had been in a blackout. Since that time she has celebrated nine happy holidays. What good is a holiday celebration if you can't remember it?

Don't consider yourself deprived if you are unable to drink the way others do. You can have a happy holiday and remember it. Others will very likely behave foolishly and feel miserable, and the only saving grace will be that they will not remember it.

God Finds Us In Many Ways
🍒

We come to believe in various ways.

A gentleman in the treatment center refused to attend the required in-house AA meetings, insisting that coercing him to participate in a "religious" program was a violation of his constitutional rights. Since he was otherwise completely cooperative in treatment, he was granted the exception.

During his third week, he entered an ongoing meeting. He stated that he had been sitting in his room, looking at the beautiful trees in the adjacent wooded area, and had been reflecting on how his life had been utterly ruined by his alcoholism. He then found himself wondering, "How come the trees out there are so beautiful and majestic? Who is taking care of them?" He then decided, "Whoever it is that is looking after those trees is certainly doing a helluva better job than I am," and then decided he would join the meeting.

The God of our understanding may be the one who looks after the trees or keeps the planets in their orbits. The serious threat of humanity becoming extinct is not because of acts of God, but because of the behavior of humans. Turning our life over to the will of the God that maintains the universe is far safer than following the dictates of human volition, which are often closer to brute passion than to human will.

Prayer Cannot Be Self-Centered
🍎

Prayer is not the same as plea bargaining.

Many people with years of recovery describe how their prayers have evolved as their sobriety has increased in quality. Initially, prayer was bargaining: "I'll be good, God, if You will do thus and so for me." When these requests were not satisfied, God had clearly not kept His side of the bargain, and therefore they were released from their obligations. It was not until much later that they stopped bargaining and their prayer turned into "Help me to do what is right. Show me the way."

When we bargain in prayer, our goal is to achieve whatever we want for ourselves; if we believe that God can provide it, we are willing to pay the price He requests. This is totally self-centered, and God becomes just another means for self-gratification. But mature prayer occurs when we yield our desires and turn our will over to God. As Step Eleven says, "Pray only for knowledge of His will for us and the power to carry that out."

Working Step Eleven is not easy. It is conceivable that God's will for us may not include the speedboat or the vacation of our dreams. A loyal soldier who goes out on a mission does so in obedience to his commander, whose wishes may be much different than his own.

Give Yourself a Break

If we desire success, we must provide a conducive environment.

It has been said, "If you have found that opportunity hasn't knocked, perhaps you had better build a door." We may complain of a lack of success without realizing that we have not made it possible.

A recovering alcoholic related that after he lost his job as chief executive officer of a company owing to his drinking, he would sit in the bar drinking, expecting that at any moment a headhunter would walk through the door to recruit him as CEO for a Fortune 500 company. It never dawned on him that a company in need of a CEO would not look for one in a bar.

While there is no guarantee that sobriety would result in his obtaining the desired position, there is at least the possibility that if he were sober and productive, and could demonstrate his organizational and administrative capacities, the opportunity just might knock. By drinking he had torn down the door, and opportunity could not knock even if it wished to.

Using chemicals certainly deters opportunity, but even in abstinence, we must behave in ways that provide a door at which opportunity can knock.

Silent Approval
🍎

As precious as silence is, failure to speak up is often taken as approval.

Families and friends of people who abuse chemicals often keep their silence, sometimes for fear that saying something will aggravate the situation, provoke the person, or rupture the relationship. They are not aware that failure to speak up is interpreted by the addict as tacit approval.

Children of an alcoholic father have said, "I could understand my father's behavior, because alcohol was affecting his brain. It was my mother's tolerance of his drinking that baffled me."

Or, "Of what use will my protesting be? He is not going to change, and it will only cause a hassle." Not quite true. The addict may indeed be provoked and may not change, but voicing your disapproval is one of the ingredients necessary to tip the scale in favor of sobriety.

"He who justifies wrongful behavior . . . is an abomination to God"—Proverbs 17:15. We do not have to be an outspoken advocate for injustice. But silence in the face of injustice is wrongful behavior.

Improvement is Always in Order

Spiritual growth never comes to an end.

The Twelve Steps of recovery are both similar and dissimilar to an escalator. They are dissimilar in that we cannot stand still but must expend effort to ascend. They are similar in that the highest step soon becomes the lowest step, as the conveyor follows a cyclical movement.

When we reach the Twelfth Step of recovery, we should go back to the First Step. As we grow in sobriety, our sense of humility should increase, and we should be able to have greater awareness of our powerlessness.

We are now approaching December 31—365 days of improvement on our character defects. Being on a higher level of spirituality shows things previously acceptable are really character defects that are no longer acceptable. With new furniture in the living room, the old drapes must be replaced. As our character improves, we can go back to character traits that had been improved upon and see how they now need refinement to bring them into line with our new level of spirituality.

How wonderful that spiritual growth does not have an endpoint. As long as we live, we have a goal toward which to strive.

True Resolutions

There is a way to make resolutions work.

Everyone jokes about New Year's resolutions because everyone makes them and no one keeps them. Some people say: "I will never take another drink," or "I will never shoot dope again." They may be sincere when they make these resolutions, but they just do not work.

The common denominator of failed resolutions is that they invariably include the word *never*. "I will never drink, or never shoot dope again." Or if not *never*, then the resolution is made for a much longer time than most people can manage.

The ideal time for human resolve is *one day*—maybe even only an hour or even less. To make a resolution for *never* or a certain number of months is setting yourself up for failure. We can no more take on that length of time than we can fly by flapping our arms.

"One day at a time" is advisable for abstinence from chemicals as well as for everything else we set our minds to do. This applies not only to other addictions such as gambling or food but also to other behavior. "I can be courteous *today*. I can avoid responding in anger *today*. I can yield the right of way *today*. I can do the dishes *today*. I can forgo some personal pleasures *today*."

Our resolutions can last, if we make them for just one day at a time.